FREEDOM
OF THE SKIES

US Army AH-64A Apache

FREEDOM OF THE SKIES

AN ILLUSTRATED HISTORY OF FIFTY YEARS OF NATO AIRPOWER

PETER R. MARCH

CASSELL

Cassell & Co.
Wellington House
125 Strand
London WC2R 0BB

First published 1999
in association with the Royal Air Force Benevolent Fund

A CIP catalogue record for this book is available from the British Library
ISBN 0-304-35238-1

Cover photograph:
A USAFE F-15E Strike Eagle from the 48th Fighter Wing heading for a mission over Bosnia.
© *Jeremy Flack/Aviation Photographs International*

Book design by: Graham Finch
Printed in France

CONTENTS

PREFACE

Half a century has passed since the North Atlantic Treaty Organisation was formed. With the Berlin Airlift coming to its end, the Western nations faced a dangerous and bleak situation in 1949 as the Soviet Union strove to dominate Europe. The 16 countries saw that the only way to face up to the growing power of communism was to build a unified defence that could match the forces facing them to the east. In this book, I have attempted to tell the story of NATO's airpower over five decades, as it became the key to maintaining international peace in Europe.

In 1949, most of NATO's air arms were equipped with aircraft that had survived from World War 2, and these were slowly being replaced by the first generation of jet-powered aircraft. Spurred on by threats and intimidation from the Soviet Union and its eastern European allies, NATO fought a long and demanding Cold War, during which technological advancement played a major part. Military aircraft, weapons, electronic warfare, missiles, avionics, command and control systems and satellites developed out of all recognition, with each side trying to keep one step ahead of the other. NATO's air arms were at the forefront throughout, with airpower holding the key to eventual success. This came with the sudden collapse of the Soviet Union, the end of the Warsaw Pact and the re-unification of Germany.

No sooner had the Cold War ended than NATO found itself facing a very different and yet more difficult situation in the strife-ridden former Yugoslavia. In the 1990s, politicians and military personnel have been presented with a series of seemingly impossible tasks, helping to restore and maintain peace in Croatia, Bosnia, Serbia and more recently, Kosovo. As a direct result of this intervention, NATO's air arms have been called into collective action for the first time and have shown that airpower has a crucial part to play in bringing – and returning – warring parties to the conference table. Peace-keeping has proved to be as complex to plan and effect as open warfare in this technological age.

Inevitably, in looking at the aircraft and role of NATO's air arms, from the Mustang and Sabre of 50 years ago to today's Fighting Falcon and Tornado, I have focused on the enormous advances in military aviation in just half a century. Whichever aspect you look at – speed, range, weapons, manoeuvrability, stealthiness, avionics, or even their appearance – you cannot but be impressed by the changes that have occurred in military aircraft in such a short time. I have tried to illustrate this in words and pictures, putting it into the context of NATO's quest for 'freedom of the skies' through the latter half of this century.

I am indebted to Ben Dunnell for his painstaking and detailed research into so many aspects of this book. The material that he produced could have easily filled two volumes, even before any photographs were added. Surprisingly, NATO itself has not kept a photographic record through much of its history, and little of what does exist is aviation orientated. I am therefore particularly grateful to Michael Bowyer, Tim Ripley, Richard Ward, Peter Foster, Paul Jackson, James Oughton, Lindsay Peacock, Brian Strickland, Jeremy Flack and Bob Archer for access to their photographic collections.

As a graphic designer and photographer, Graham Finch is able to draw on his detailed knowledge of aviation to present the words and pictures in a most attractive way, and he has been of immense help through the final stages of this book.

To the many other people who have supplied information and photographs for *Freedom of the Skies* – thank you.

PETER R. MARCH
April 1999

FORMATION

US Air Force Lockheed P-80 Shooting Stars

FORMATION

After Victory in Europe was celebrated on 8 May 1945, the realisation that new peacetime challenges and demands confronted the Western Allies was not long in coming. The signing of the United Nations Charter, in June of that year in San Francisco, established the first of the new post-war alliances, as hostility from the Soviet Union beckoned, and then reared its head. The next four years further hardened the attitudes of the West against the communist threat, as the USSR began to expand its influence further into Europe, with clear consequences for the defensive arrangements of its wartime allies.

The former Prime Minister, Winston Churchill (defeated by the Labour Party led by Clement Attlee in the 1945 general election) in Fulton, Missouri during March 1946, spoke of "an Iron Curtain... descending across the continent of Europe", summing up the mood of resignation towards the situation at the time. Supported by the Soviets, communist rule in Poland began after the country's general election in January 1947. This was followed just over a year later by a successful communist coup in Czechoslovakia. In presenting his so-called 'Truman Doctrine' to Congress in 1947, American President Harry S. Truman implored the USA to "support free peoples who are resisting attempted subjugation by armed minorities or by outside pressure". This was a clear sign of the already mounting opposition to Stalin and his allies by the Western powers, amongst whom there was a growing feeling that what was needed was a form of collaborative union between nations, taking defence as a leading priority.

Left: A large fleet of Douglas C-47 Skytrains was deployed to Europe by the USAF for Operation Vittles in 1948-49.

The arrival in Europe of funds from the Marshall Aid plan, as proposed by US Secretary of State George Marshall in June 1947, soon began to assist post-war regeneration and underlined the USA's commitment to the region. In Europe itself, the British Foreign Secretary Ernest Bevin proposed the foundation of a Western European Union. On 17 March 1948, the Brussels Treaty was signed by the foreign ministers of Belgium, France, Luxembourg, the Netherlands and the United Kingdom, establishing the first formal defensive ties. These were strengthened by the Convention for European Co-operation, which followed a month later. This embraced 16 countries and the Commanders-in-Chief of the Western Zones of Occupation in Germany.

The first significant post-war test of the West's resolve came in June 1948, with the start of the Soviet blockade of Berlin. Within two days of its imposition, the request from the American Military Governor of Germany, General Lucius D Clay, for an airlift of supplies, had been met by US Air Forces in Europe (USAFE). The Berlin Airlift became a joint task force, with the Royal Air Force (RAF) and civilian operators participating in the effort, under the US title Operation *Vittles*. Alongside the C-47 Skytrains, C-54 Skymasters and other transports that were being deployed to Europe from the USA, were increased numbers of front-line operational aircraft, as the Cold War began to intensify. USAF Strategic Air Command B-29 Superfortresses

arrived in Britain in July 1948, and were soon joined by F-80 Shooting Stars from two USAF Fighter Groups. They were deployed to augment the F-51D Mustangs and RAF Hawker Tempests already providing fighter cover for the airlift, as instances of Soviet fighters 'buzzing' Allied transports in transit through the air corridors continued to occur.

This was an especially opportune time for talks on North Atlantic defence to commence in Washington, a June 1948 meeting bringing together the USA, Canada and the five signatory countries of the Brussels Treaty. These nations (Belgium, France, Luxembourg, the Netherlands and the UK) announced the creation of a Western Union Defence Organisation in September. This was a positive move towards firm defensive provision for the region against the growing threat from the East.

Following the Washington talks on 25-26 October 1948, the Brussels Treaty countries announced 'complete agreement on the principle of a defensive pact for the North Atlantic and on the next steps to be taken in this direction'. It was not long before representatives of these nations, together with Canada and the USA met again to begin the drafting process for the new North Atlantic Treaty. After three months, the governments of Denmark, Iceland, Italy, Norway and Portugal were invited to join in the Treaty discussions, and its final text was published on 18 March 1949. The twelve nations signed the document in Washington on 4 April, establishing the North Atlantic Treaty Organisation – NATO.

Above: The RAF's new Handley Page Hastings transport was pressed into service in Germany to assist with the huge airlift.

Left: Amongst the fighters that patrolled the busy air corridors to Berlin were RAF Hawker Tempests, ready to ward off Soviet fighters sent up to harass the Allied transports.

When NATO officially came into being in April 1949, the USAF already had a large force in Europe, including two wings of F-80s (right).

European air arms relied heavily on wartime piston-engined aircraft like this Belgian Air Force Spitfire (above) and French Navy Lancaster (right).

Key to the alliance's declared defensive purpose is Article 5 of the Treaty:

'The parties agree that an armed attack against one or more of them in Europe or North America should be considered an attack against them all, and consequently they agree that, if such an armed attack occurs, each of them, in the exercise of the right of individual collective self-defence recognised by Article 51 of the Charter of the United Nations, will assist the party or parties so attacked by taking forthwith, individually and in concert with other parties, such action as it deems necessary, including the use of armed force, to restore and maintain the security of the North Atlantic area'.

Berlin still remained the focus of attention, with the Airlift reaching its peak on 16 April 1949 with the so-called 'Easter Parade' that saw 12,940 tons of vital cargo being delivered during the course of 1,398 sorties. This was a significant morale-boosting effort, both for those directly involved with the Airlift and the people of Berlin. Already, the resolve of all had been tested during the harsh 1948-49 winter, but both then and with April's 'big push', a clear signal was sent to the Soviets that the Allies were not about to capitulate in the city.

Since the North Atlantic Treaty did not actually come into force until 24 August 1949, the end of the Soviet blockade on 12 May could not be said to be a

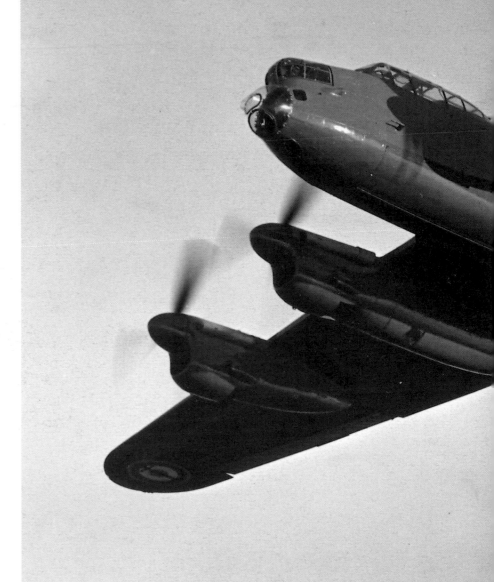

direct result of the new alliance. Nevertheless, the West had stood firm throughout the Berlin episode, and the Airlift itself had been enough to withstand the huge potential risks to the security of the whole of western Europe. It continued to operate until 30 September 1949, by which time some 2,325 million tons of food, fuel and other equipment had been supplied by the US Air Force, US Navy, RAF and Commonwealth air arms, as well as civilian operators, to the beleaguered city.

1949 was a very significant year in terms of developments made to create new alliances and political structures in Europe. The first session of the Council of Europe was held in Strasbourg in August, while in September the Constitution of the Federal Republic of Germany was established. A month later, the east-west division of the country was made complete by the establishment of a separate state, the German Democratic Republic (DDR), no solution having been reached for the future of Germany as a whole, by the Conference of Foreign Ministers in Paris that summer.

The situation in Berlin may have been eased, but fears continued regarding the presence of a communist government so close to the heart of western Europe and the possibilities of aggression emanating from further east. This was especially worrying in view of the considerably larger military strength of the USSR, that had not been cut back after World War 2, unlike the forces of its former

Above: USAF Boeing B-29 Superfortresses were first deployed to Europe in 1948, with an increasing number being based in Britain and Germany through 1949 and 1950.

Left: DH Vampires, the first jet aircraft to be introduced into French Air Force service, were built as the Mistral by SNCASE.

allies. The announcement by President Truman in September 1949 that USAF WB-29s carrying out air sampling sorties had detected evidence of the first Soviet nuclear test (held on 29 August that year) was obviously significant – the arms race had commenced.

These 'weather reconnaissance flights' were part of a steadily growing number of flights being carried out by US military aircraft along the USSR's borders. They included many electronic intelligence (ELINT)-gathering sorties over the Baltic by US Navy Consolidated PB4Y Privateers, normally based at Port Lyautey in French Morocco, but detached for these clandestine missions to Wiesbaden AB, Germany. One of these aircraft was the victim of the first Cold War shootdown. On 8 April 1950, a Privateer from US Navy Squadron VP-26, flying near

Leyaya, Latvia, was destroyed by Soviet fighters, with the loss of all ten crew on board. This prompted an 'official ban' on further penetrations of Soviet airspace.

In theory, NATO and its provision for mutual defence led by the US, as set out in the 'Truman Doctrine', provided immediate support for the re-arming of European forces. However, the Western Union, with the UK as its major participant, still led the way forward at first. The British Government had supplied such wartime types as the Avro Lancaster (to France in the maritime reconnaissance role) and Supermarine Spitfire, to fellow WU members. These were followed by examples of the first British jet fighters, the Gloster Meteor and de Havilland Vampire.

Of these, the Meteor F4 and T7 were flown in some numbers by the Royal Netherlands Air Force from 1948, prior to production of the improved Meteor F8 at the Fokker factory in Amsterdam. Along with Avions Fairey, the Dutch firm also supplied Meteor F8s to the Belgian Air Force, where they replaced Gloster-built F4s, while the other early WU and NATO user of this pioneering jet fighter was Denmark.

The Vampire was supplied to France's Armée de l'Air prior to being license-built by SNCASE at Marignane, 328 being operated from 1949. The Italian Aeronautica Militare Italiana also selected the Vampire as its first new post-WW2 combat aircraft, built both by the manufacturer and by FIAT and Macchi as FB52As, while NF54 night-fighters followed. Vampire F3s and FB52s served with five units of the Royal Norwegian Air Force from 1948, and Portugal purchased Vampires for training.

Although mutual defence was central to NATO's operation, in 1949 the armed forces of the signatory countries were still being rebuilt and restructured to cope with the new demands of the post-war climate. In April of that year requests had been made to the USA by all of the other member states, for American military and financial assistance. This was soon put into effect under the terms of the 1949 Mutual Defence Assistance Act, signed by US President Harry S. Truman on 6 October. In January 1950, the US government released some $900 million of military aid funds, that soon proved to be the key that opened the door for the re-equipment of NATO's armed forces.

The US Air Force's European-based presence,

Left: The Royal Norwegian
Air Force equipped five
front-line squadrons with
the DH Vampire FB52
(illustrated) and the NF54
night-fighter.

Avro Lincolns were flown
by RAF Bomber Command
through the early years of
NATO. Some were replaced
by Boeing B-29 Washingtons,
as an interim measure.

under the control of USAFE, had steadily increased since the arrival of the first B-29 Superfortress deployments to Britain and Germany in 1948. Several stations in eastern England continued to receive regular temporary duty (TDY) stays by B-29s and the improved Boeing B-50s of Strategic Air Command, while the USAF's ability to make long-range deployments was clearly demonstrated with a series of impressive ferry flights for the re-equipment of USAFE units. For example, in September-October 1950, 180 F-84E Thunderjets were flown across the Atlantic to bases in Germany. Further B-29s arrived in Europe during 1950 as new equipment for eight squadrons of RAF Bomber Command. Designated the Washington B1, the B-29 was a stop-gap bomber while the RAF waited for the turbo-jet powered Canberra to enter service. Prior to this, all but two of the RAF's heavy bomber squadrons flew the Avro Lincoln B2, while the three medium bomber units in Europe (two in the UK and one at Celle in Germany) used de Havilland Mosquito B35s.

As a result of the Mutual Defence Assistance Program (MDAP), funding was now available to further the post-war re-equipment programmes of all of the NATO air arms in Europe. The new alliance's key defensive role was brought into focus by events in Korea, where the conflict, which began in June 1950, involved US, British and Commonwealth forces ranged against the Soviet-supported North Korean forces, underlining the reality of the communist threat around the world. At this time, the WU still had the greater defensive burden in Europe on its shoulders, staging international military exercises for the first time in August 1950, but NATO soon began to assume its military role.

Defence planning in the Organisation's area of influence gathered pace. In the eastern Mediterranean, Greece and Turkey made their initial steps towards joining NATO, by affiliation to its

USAF Strategic Air Command replaced its B-29s with the improved B-50 in 1950, for its temporary detachments to Europe, while awaiting the introduction of the B-47 Stratojet.

Right: USAFE's first major jet fighter re-equipment came in the autumn of 1950, when 180 Republic F-84E Thunderjets were flown to bases in West Germany.

Main picture: With funding from the Mutual Defence Assistance Program (MDAP), European air arms soon began to re-equip their fighter squadrons with jet aircraft like the Gloster Meteor and F-84 Thunderjet, shown here in Belgian Air Force markings.

military agencies, and French Prime Minister René Pleven's proposal for a unified European army, to include West Germany, led to further discussions on defensive matters within NATO and the North Atlantic Council. Not least of the vital issues was the question of Germany's future involvement, the topic of the Petersberg negotiations late in 1950. The thought of 'a Korea' happening in Europe had been one of the reasons for NATO assuming the military role in place of the Western Union. Formally agreed on 20 December 1950, this resulted in the military organisation of the WU being dissolved as a separate entity, and merged into NATO.

The pivotal role of the USA within NATO was underlined by the North Atlantic Council's choice of General Dwight D Eisenhower for the post of Supreme Allied Commander Europe (SACEUR) in December 1950. US General Eisenhower, who had led the Allied offensive against Nazi Germany from 1944, was of course very familiar with the European theatre of operations. A growing number of staff – initially Americans, but soon including personnel from other NATO nations – started to come together in temporary offices at the Hotel Astoria in Paris, already home to a US military communications detachment. Supreme Headquarters Allied Powers Europe (SHAPE) officially became operational,

along with Allied Command Europe (ACE), on 2 April 1951. It comprised 183 officers from nine of the then twelve NATO member countries, but with the majority from the USA. A headquarters building was already under construction at a new location at this time, and both SHAPE and ACE transferred to Rocquencourt in the Versailles district of Paris on 23 July 1951. ACE's area of responsibility was divided into three – north-west, central and southern Europe, each with its own subordinate commands for ground, sea and air forces.

Major increases in US defence spending from 1951 onwards, up to a budget of some $50 million, were intended to enhance significantly its ability to project power globally. As part of NATO's military build-up, which was now gathering pace, five US Army divisions were to be based in Europe as well as more USAFE front-line aircraft. These moves spurred on increases by the other NATO member countries in their military involvement helped by the US Marshall Aid programme. Gen. Eisenhower's efforts from the beginning of his tenure as SACEUR were directed towards major improvements in

After entering service in 1949, the swept-wing MiG-15 went on to replace piston-engined fighters with the air forces of most communist states in Europe.

NATO's military capability. Both Britain and France, for example, added a third to their defence budgets in 1951, while NATO's overall spending level increased year-on-year to the tune of some $20 million over the period 1951 to 1953.

On the other side of Europe, similar steps were being taken, with the USSR adopting an increasingly threatening posture. The Soviet Air Forces were retiring their piston-engined fighters like the Yakovlev Yak-9 and Lavochkin La-9/11, and were introducing the new Mikoyan-Gurevich MiG-15 into service with regiments based both at home and in other Eastern Bloc countries. Deliveries of the MiG-15bis version commenced in 1949, which like the USAF's F-86 Sabre, saw its first combat action in Korea during 1950. Licence production of MiG-15s was undertaken in Poland by WSK, and in Czechoslovakia by Letov, equipping both of these countries' air forces. Soviet-built examples were flown by the Bulgarian, East German, Hungarian and Romanian air arms. MiG-15s were supplied in large numbers, particularly to East Germany where Soviet units (forming part of the 22 Divisions of the Group of Soviet Forces in Germany) augmented

those of the DDR's LSK/LV. The deployment of more modern NATO combat jets became an increasingly urgent priority.

In Central Europe, two NATO Allied Tactical Air Forces were established in 1952 as part of its new military structures – the 2nd ATAF to the north, with the RAF at its forefront, albeit still awaiting more modern equipment, and the 4th ATAF in the south, with its largest contributor being the USAF. In February that same year Greece and Turkey were admitted to membership, strengthening its southern flank, while later in 1952 further measures were taken towards the accession of the Federal Republic of Germany to the Treaty, as it became part of the newly-formed European Defence Community. When the Allied occupation of Germany officially ended in October 1954, the way was then clear for this important step to be taken. West Germany became a NATO member on 5 May 1955 – only nine days before the USSR formed the Warsaw Pact between itself and Albania, Bulgaria, Czechoslovakia, East Germany, Hungary, Poland and Romania. The road to confrontation between East and West was well and truly laid.

Five RAF Bomber Command squadrons received Boeing B-29 Washingtons, while waiting for the introduction into service of the English Electric Canberra jet bomber.

AIRPOWER EXPANDS

US Air Force North American F-86 Sabre

U.S. AIR FORCE
25116

NX3145T

FU-116

AIRPOWER EXPANDS

American funding, through the Offshore Procurement programme, assisted the manufacture of more modern combat aircraft in Europe to supply NATO forces in the early 1950s. As a result, British-built Armstrong Whitworth Meteor night-fighters went to Belgium, Denmark and France as well as the RAF, while the first post-war fighter design of France's own aircraft industry, the Dassault MD450 Ouragan, entered Armée de l'Air service in 1952 as a Vampire replacement.

At the same time NATO's air arms began to be supplied with American equipment, under the provisions of MDAP, for training as well as front-line service, heralding the start of the major expansion of the air power assets. Among the first aircraft to be provided were Lockheed T-33As for use as advanced and operational trainers, joining the inventories of Belgium, Canada (built by Canadair as the CT-133 Silver Star), Denmark, France, West Germany, Greece, Italy, the Netherlands, Norway and Turkey. Of the NATO nations with air arms in the mid-1950s, only the RAF chose not to equip with T-33s,

Above: The first indigenous jet fighter to go into production in France was the Dassault Ouragan, illustrated, which led to the improved Mystère.

Below: A Royal Danish Air Force Lockheed T-33A, a type that was widely used by European air arms for advanced and operational training.

Left: The RAF's contribution to the Second Allied Tactical Air Force in Germany was at first principally the DH Vampire, followed by the DH Venom, shown here.

preferring instead to operate the 'home-grown' de Havilland Vampire T11 and Gloster Meteor T7.

Many front-line NATO units in mainland Europe also received the Republic F-84F Thunderstreak at a relatively early stage in the MDAP – 1,301 examples of the machine serving in Belgium, Denmark, France, West Germany, Greece, Italy, the Netherlands, Norway and Turkey in the fighter-bomber role. The reconnaissance RF-84F Thunderflash was also common to all these air forces, becoming NATO's most numerous tactical

recce asset during this decade, with 386 being supplied. In particular, the Thunderstreak and Thunderflash provided the re-established West German Luftwaffe with the backbone of its front-line force committed to NATO, two squadrons using the F-84F. In their various derivatives, the T-33 and F-84 became almost standard equipment for the alliance at the time, although the latter was rather more a 'stop-gap' whilst waiting for the next generation of combat aircraft types to become available from the USA.

Left: NATO's main fighter reconnaissance aircraft became the Republic RF-84F Thunderflash, after nearly 400 were supplied to air arms across Europe, such as the Royal Danish Air Force, illustrated here.

A Belgian Air Force F-84F Thunderstreak, one of over 1,300 of the type flown by nine NATO forces.

The RAF continued with British designs during the early 1950s, the major part of its day fighter and fighter-bomber inventory comprising the Gloster Meteor F8, the de Havilland Vampire and later the de Havilland Venom. However, in May 1951 the entry of the English Electric Canberra into service with No 101 Squadron at RAF Binbrook, made the RAF the first air force in Europe and only the second in the world (after the USAF, with the B-45 Tornado) to be equipped with jet bombers. Four squadrons of Canberras were formed as part of the

Second Allied Tactical Air Force (2ATAF) at RAF Gütersloh, West Germany, from October 1954.

Apart from the USA and Canada, the RAF was the first NATO air arm to acquire North American F-86 Sabres under MDAP. A total of 430 Canadair-built CL-13 (F-86E) Sabre F4s were delivered, starting in December 1952, to fill the gap between the retirement of some Meteors and Vampires, mostly with 2 ATAF in Germany, and the arrival in service of Britain's first swept-wing fighters, the Hawker Hunter and Supermarine Swift.

Britain's first jet bomber, the English Electric Canberra was airborne for the first time on 13 May 1949, and entered RAF service two years later.

The RAF received Canadair-built F-86E Sabre F4s from December 1952 as Meteor and Vampire replacements, before the Hunter and Swift entered service.

Sabres had equipped several Royal Canadian Air Force (RCAF) wings in Europe from late 1951, being based in Britain, France and West Germany. However, the first examples of the type to be stationed in the theatre had been a relatively small number of USAF F-86As, but the cessation of hostilities in Korea allowed newer F-86Fs to be deployed from mid-1953. They replaced F-84G Thunderjets in three fighter wings, once more being stationed at British, French and West German bases. These were followed by two fighter-bomber wings of F-86H Sabres that were based in France. By now, SAC's Boeing B-29 and B-50 visits had been

enhanced by the new Convair B-36 and the first examples of the Boeing B-47 Stratojet. They increased the Command's hemispheric conventional and nuclear capability quite appreciably. The strategy at this time, in the event of a Soviet strike, as laid down at the Lisbon NATO conference in February 1952, was for the Allied ground forces to 'hold out' for three days at most, prior to SAC commencing a nuclear attack against selected cities in the USSR.

The frequency of the SAC deployments intensified through the 1950s as east-west tension heightened. At the same time the RAF bolstered the strategic jet nuclear bomber fleet available to NATO, with the service debut of the Vickers Valiant in 1955. This was the first of the triumvirate of 'V-bombers' to reach Bomber Command's squadrons – followed by the Victor and Vulcan – that were operated in the strategic bomber and long-range reconnaissance roles. SAC itself received the B-52 Stratofortress in June 1955, starting a new era for both the Command and the US Air Force, and if required, could provide NATO with a still greater potential to respond to Soviet aggression.

USAF and RCAF Sabres made up part of the 4th Allied Tactical Air Force, alongside the French Air Force's Commandement Aérien Tactique (Tactical Air Command). The Armée de l'Air itself began replacing its Ouragans with new Dassault Mystères, again assisted by the Offshore Procurement scheme. The new fighters were superior in performance over both their predecessor and the F-84s that were also in the AdlA inventory at this time.

With the 2nd ATAF, the RAF began receiving its first British-built swept-wing fighters in July 1954, with delivery of the Supermarine Swift F1 and Hawker Hunter F1. Unfortunately, both types were found to be inadequate in service with RAF Fighter Command and did not equip NATO-assigned squadrons until improved versions became available. The Hunter subsequently saw the widest service and development after its early teething troubles were cured. The Swift's problems continued however, and the fighter marks had a limited life in the inventory. The Swift FR5, the first serving RAF aircraft to use an afterburning engine, entered service in the tactical reconnaissance role with the 2nd ATAF in 1956. Nearly 100 FR5s saw rather more successful employment with NATO, all being based in Germany.

The Hunter quickly became the RAF's primary air defence fighter, initially with the F4 in the mid-1950s and subsequently the further improved F6.

First of the RAF's trio of 'V-bombers', the Vickers Valiant entered service as a strategic bomber in 1955, but all were withdrawn by 1965 after the discovery of chronic fatigue problems.

The mighty Convair RB-36E was used by the USAF for high altitude, long-range reconnaissance, before its replacement by the faster and more capable RB-47 Stratojet.

SAC's main contribution through the 1950s was the deployment of its front-line bomber squadrons' B-47 Stratojets to UK bases. This aircraft is fitted with JATO bottles, for assisted take-off with a heavy bomb load in high temperatures.

RAF Hunters participated in 1956's major Exercises *Rejuvenate* and *Stronghold*, during which the type demonstrated its high-altitude interception capability against simulated attacks by USAF B-47 Stratojets of SAC units on deployment, and RAF Valiants and Canberras. At around this time, the new Canberra B(I)8 was entering service as the specialist intruder/attack version of the jet bomber, beginning with No 88 Squadron at RAF Wildenrath.

With the 2nd ATAF, Hunter F4s went to West German-based wings as replacements for stop-gap Sabres and the ageing Venoms. A high state of alert was maintained by the fighter squadrons, with two aircraft on immediate standby and all others in each unit at 15 minutes' readiness. This Zulu alert posture was also maintained by the USAF and Canadian Sabres, and French Ouragans and Mystères that made up most of the 4th ATAF's air defence assets further south.

While the RAF was relinquishing its Sabres, the type was making its debut with other air arms in mainland Europe under the auspices of the MDAP, primarily as an F-84 replacement. A USAF Air Materiel Command requirement for a basic all-weather fighter, to be built under license by local manufacturers for NATO, was met by the F-86K Sabre (a derivative of the USAF's F-86D). The first aircraft were built by North American, with initial deliveries to Royal Netherlands Air Force and Royal Norwegian Air Force units in 1955, prior to Fiat in Italy starting production in Turin. F-86Ks were supplied to the French, West German and Italian Air Forces, of which the Luftwaffe was the largest user, with 88 equipping one Jagdgeschwader.

After the USAF, RCAF and RAF started to replace their Sabre day-fighters, these F-86s were passed on to other NATO air forces, the first recipient being Turkey, whose Canadair-built machines started to arrive in 1954 for three squadrons, with F-86Ds adding an all-weather capability five years later. In 1956-57, Italy received 188 ex-RAF Sabre 4s that went to three AMI bases. These would only have been directly assigned to NATO as air defenders in wartime, the F-84G remaining the backbone of Italy's commitment. F-86Fs became the second Sabre version in Norwegian service from 1957 onwards, 115 providing the KNL with a much-needed extension

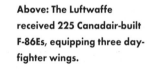

Above: The Luftwaffe received 225 Canadair-built F-86Es, equipping three day-fighter wings.

Left: MDAP funds enabled many NATO air forces to re-equip with F-86 Sabres, including the all-weather F-86D/K versions, shown here in service with the Norwegian Air Force.

of its interceptor capability. NATO's principal F-86 user in Europe was West Germany. All of its 225 aircraft were Canadair-built, most being Sabre 6s that equipped three units, the first post-WW2 Luftwaffe day-fighter wings, while the Mk5 was used for operational training.

The Royal Canadian Air Force progressively replaced its Sabres based in Europe with an improved all-weather air defence capability being offered by four squadrons of Avro Canada CF-100 Mk4Bs. These big, twin-jets were transferred from Air Defense Command and further CF-100 Canuck Mk5s were supplied to the Belgian Air Force, where they re-equipped three squadrons. The supply of these Canucks was again largely paid for under MDAP arrangements. A much-needed, improved all-weather capability for the RAF was provided by the Gloster Javelin, that equipped front-line squadrons in the UK and Germany, the first aircraft arriving with the 2nd ATAF in August 1957.

The Hawker Hunter became a key
fighter in the RAF's and NATO's
inventory. This is a formation of
Hunter F6s from No 14 Squadron
over West Germany in 1960.

At this time the USAF made a significant step forward in Europe, where it started to replace its F-86 Sabres with the new F-100C Super Sabre with Wings based in the UK, France and Germany. While this aircraft was an air superiority fighter with a secondary fighter-bomber role, the following F-100D was a dedicated fighter-bomber whose weapon-carrying and delivery systems were much improved. As the Super Sabre became USAFE's most numerically-important front-line asset, marking a significant step forward for this NATO air arm's capabilities within the Alliance, so the Cold War began to heighten. This made further enhancements to NATO's wider defensive and offensive assets all the more important, as the threat of direct Soviet aggression against the Western powers grew. In 1956, the Suez crisis involving NATO partners France and Britain, and an attempted revolution in Hungary, caused yet further east-west tension. The strengthening of NATO's defensive and retaliatory capabilites with the introduction of improved aircraft and weapons, largely funded under MDAP, was a critical factor in preventing the Cold War escalating into military action.

Replacing F-86s, the USAF's supersonic North American F-100 was based in Britain, France and Germany. These Super Sabres are in the colours of the 20th Tactical Fighter Wing's 79th Tactical Fighter Squadron.

The first delta-wing jet fighter, the Gloster Javelin replaced the RAF's Meteor NF12/14s with all-weather, day/night air defence squadrons.

23363

THE COLD WAR INTENSIFIES

US Air Force B-47E Stratojet

THE COLD WAR INTENSIFIES

In August 1957, the US and Canadian Air Defense Commands were integrated into the new North American Air Defense System (NORAD), with its headquarters at Colorado Springs. This was an important development in the light of the growing possibility of an attack from the Soviet Union on the American mainland. During April of the following year, another clear signal was sent to the Soviets, when NATO's defence ministers met in Paris to re-affirm the Alliance's defensive posture. This followed the launch of the Sputnik satellite by the USSR during October 1957, an event which came as a great bombshell to the rest of the world. The fear that now gripped western leaders was that the Soviet Union, in possessing this technology, was embarking upon a programme of nuclear development which was about to overtake,

or was already ahead of, US, French or British space and missile technology.

Significant advances in terms of the nuclear deterrent available to NATO continued to be made. For its part, the RAF's 'V-force' was being built up through 1956-57, as first the Avro Vulcan, and then the Handley Page Victor, began to reach Bomber Command squadrons in greater numbers. These enhanced the detachments of USAF SAC B-47 Stratojets that continued to spend 45-day periods at Greenham Common, Brize Norton, Fairford and Upper Heyford. Numerous major exercises tested the operational effectiveness of the respective services' strategic bomber inventories, as well as their ability to work in conjunction with fighter and fighter-bomber assets. RAF Valiants, Victors and Vulcans participated annually in SAC's bombing

Right: A line-up of delta-winged Avro Vulcan strategic bombers, a type that flew in RAF service through three decades.

Below: The crescent-winged Handley Page Victor B1 was the third of the RAF's 'V-bombers'.

Right: SAC's heavy bomber, the B-52 Stratofortress, was not based in Europe, but made frequent training flights across the Atlantic, like this example seen at RAF Greenham Common.

Left: A McDonnell F-101
fighter-bomber, flown by
the 81st Tactical Fighter
Wing, seen landing at RAF
Bentwaters in August 1959.

Continuing the upgrade of its front-line aircraft in Europe, USAFE received its first Voodoos in 1958. The RF-101C version played an important part in tactical reconnaissance.

competition, and the two Commands became closely integrated, thus ensuring that NATO possessed a powerful nuclear force in the event of hostilities developing. Bomber Command received American nuclear weapons for the 'V-bomber' and Canberra fleets, and was integrated into SAC's battle plan.

NATO's 'tripwire' policy of launching an instant response using bombers and missiles in the event of a Soviet attack on any member country, meant that the integration of RAF Bomber Command's and

SAC's strategic attack forces was all the more credible as a deterrent by delivering all-out nuclear retaliation. With newer B-52Ds entering service with SAC, augmenting earlier Stratofortress variants and the ageing B-47s, a new alert programme known as *Reflex Action* was initiated in 1957. This replaced the 90-day rotational training concept for forward-based SAC aircraft, and was adopted at all Forward Operating Locations (FOLs). Later, trials were conducted of a continuous airborne alert

By 1960 in the UK, the first generation B-45s had been replaced in USAF service by B-66 Destroyers, one of which is seen here.

Left: In September 1958 the USAF sent the first of its new Lockheed C-130As to Evreux, France. Over 40 years later, a squadron of Hercules (C-130Es) remains active with USAFE.

Right: The third 'century' fighter deployed to Europe was the F-102A Delta Dagger, for all-weather fighter interceptor duties. This aircraft was flown by the 496th FIS based at Hahn, West Germany.

posture using the B-52s. However, this was not adopted under regular operations.

USAFE received a major boost to its assets in 1958, with the introduction of McDonnell F-101 Voodoos for fighter-bomber and, with the F-101B, long-range interceptor duties. A further variant, the tactical reconnaissance RF-101C, later equipped one wing. Another new arrival with USAFE in the late 1950s was the Douglas B-66 Destroyer, and its reconnaissance derivative, the RB-66, both of which were based in the UK as B-45 and RB-45 Tornado replacements. USAFE units based in Germany and the Netherlands received F-102A Delta Daggers for all-weather interceptor duties, to replace their F-86 Sabres. The new generation of supersonic 'century series' jet fighters – the F-100, F-101 and F-102 – were now all serving in Europe. No less significant meanwhile was the major boost given to NATO's transport capability, when the USAF deployed its C-130A Hercules for the first time, to Evreux in France, during September 1958.

Another very important event in terms of NATO's air power came in early 1958, with the initial deliveries of the first aircraft type to be designed to a requirement issued by the Alliance

itself – the Fiat G-91, the result of the NATO Basic Military Requirement (NBMR)1 specification issued to European aircraft manufacturers in the spring of 1954. This called for a lightweight fighter/close support aircraft, of robust construction and easy to maintain, with rough-field capability and a top speed of Mach 0.92. It was intended for operation by all of the NATO air forces, carrying underwing conventional or tactical nuclear stores. After a first flight on 9 August 1956, the G-91 participated in trials at Bretigny in France the following year, and demonstrated that it met the Alliance's requirement. Among the machines rejected were the original, land-based Dassault Etendard, and the Folland Midge. The light fighter was powered by a Bristol Orpheus turbojet, itself intended to be a standard NATO powerplant (developed as a result of the initial project conference at Lisbon in 1952).

Not surprisingly, the Italian Air Force placed the first production order for the ground-attack G-91, closely followed by West Germany, France, Greece and Turkey. However, only West Germany actually took delivery of new-built aircraft, later joined by Portugal as an operator. The Greek and Turkish orders were cancelled, their aircraft being

transferred to the Luftwaffe, most of whose own aircraft were licence produced by Flugzeug-Union-Süd at Oberpfaffenhofen (a collaboration of Messerschmitt, Dornier and Heinkel), while the intended production for France was also shelved. The photo-reconnaissance G-91R/1 followed the ground-attack fighter version into service, and was evaluated by the USA. However, no further orders were forthcoming for this NATO-optimised design – a problem soon to be faced by other such programmes.

In 1959, the first F-100 Super Sabres were delivered to NATO air arms other than the USAF, led by the French Air Force, who equipped two Escadrons de Chasse with them. Others went to the Turkish Air Force (some 260 in all), and the Royal Danish Air Force (F-100Ds and two-seat F-100Fs serving with Esk 727 and Esk 730 at Skyrdstrup). All three of these operators kept their Super Sabres in service for many years.

Germany remained a particularly significant 'sticking point' between the Soviet Union and NATO. In November 1958, the new leader of the USSR, Nikita Khrushchev (who had come to power

Above: A pair of Royal Danish Air Force F-100Ds taking off from Skyrdstrup, from where two squadrons operated Super Sabres for nearly 30 years.

Above: Built to meet NATO specification NBMR-1, for a lightweight/close support fighter, the Fiat G-91 was supplied in quantity to the West German Air Force. The Luftwaffe's G-91R-3 fighter-reconnaissance version is illustrated.

Left: Supplied under MDAP, the French Air Force was the first European country to receive Super Sabres, in 1959, including a number of two-seat F-100Fs. This single-seat F-100D was photographed in 1965.

in the Kremlin eight months earlier) announced his wish to terminate the Four-Power Agreement on the status of Berlin, a proposal which was naturally rejected by the Western powers. In December, the Ministers of the North Atlantic Council declared that they supported the views of the other occupying powers – France, the UK and the USA – on this issue, leaving the question of Berlin's future totally unresolved. The West German Federal Chancellor, Konrad Adenauer, found support from the then recently-elected French President, Charles de Gaulle, for his firm stance on the city.

An increasing number of overflights of the USSR's borders and widespread electronic

intelligence (ELINT)-gathering sorties were now being flown as the threat from the East increased. This was not without the risk of retaliation by the Soviet Air Force and ground forces. A USAF C-130A-II Hercules flying out of Adana in Turkey was shot down over Armenia by five MiG-17s on 2 September 1958 with the loss of its crew, this having followed the 'downing' of numerous other SAC reconnaissance aircraft either by fighters or anti-aircraft artillery, including two RB-29s and an RB-47. The information gathered from these sorties, together with 'ground' sources, revealed the rapid development in missile technology being made by the USSR. This was of growing concern to NATO

A high-flying Lockheed U-2, similar to the aircraft in which Gary Powers was shot down over Russia on 1 May 1960.

when put alongside the increasing strength of the Soviet Air Forces and its allies.

The introduction of new surface-to-air missile (SAM) systems presented a significant threat to any aircraft penetrating Soviet airspace, and the availability to the USSR of intercontinental ballistic missiles (ICBMs) capable of hitting targets in the USA was heightening NATO's anxiety. In terms of more conventional weapons, Mikoyan MiG-21 *Fishbeds* started to enter service with Russian Frontal Aviation and the PVO's air defence regiments in 1959, progressively replacing the first generation MiG-15s, MiG-17s and MiG-19s, while Russian Long-Range Aviation received Tupolev Tu-95 *Bear* bombers, providing an extended strategic capability alongside the medium-range Myasishchev M-4 *Bison* and Tu-16 *Badger*. The Soviet threat to the West was having to be re-appraised by NATO and other defence strategists as a matter of urgency.

Tension mounted on 1 May 1960 when Soviet SAMs shot down a Lockheed U-2C being flown by CIA pilot Francis Gary Powers over Sverdlovsk,

Below: One of the specially modified reconnaissance RB-47H Stratojets that the USAF operated from RAF Upper Heyford.

The Russians made many attempts at probing NATO's air defence radar and early warning network, using a variety of aircraft that included this Tu-16 *Badger* photographed over the North Sea.

Above: Another type to be deployed to Europe by President Kennedy as part of Operation *Stair Step* was the RF-84F Thunderflash.

When the US President sent large scale reinforcements for NATO to Europe in 1961, they included Air Guard F-86H Sabres like this 102nd Wing aircraft from the Massachusetts ANG.

Russia. This halted the programme of US overflights by U-2s that had been progressing for four years. Following the announcement by Khrushchev, six days after the shootdown, that a Soviet Rocket Force Command had been established, an urgent summit meeting took place in Paris, again involving France, the UK, USA and USSR. It soon broke down and the communist governments promptly withdrew from the UN disarmament discussions that were also in progress. Exactly two months after Powers' U-2 was lost, a USAF ERB-47H fell victim to a MiG-17 while flying in international airspace over the Barents Sea.

Further tension followed in early 1961, again relating to Berlin. After the North Atlantic Council re-affirmed its 1958 stance on the city's status the previous December, the Soviet government returned again to the question of the Four-Power Agreement and Khrushchev's demand that it should be terminated. The new US President, John F Kennedy, met the Soviet leader in Vienna in June 1961, but to no avail. Khrushchev declared that a bilateral agreement on Berlin between the USSR and East Germany was imminent. The North Atlantic

Council once again laid down the areas on which the Allies were to remain absolutely firm – retaining the presence of Western troops in Berlin, maintaining unhindered access to the city, and keeping in place the economic links between West Berlin, which remained an 'island' within the DDR, and the Federal Republic itself. Numbers of refugees heading to the FRG through West Berlin, now the only door left open after stricter controls were imposed on the East-West German border, began to rise dramatically during 1961, posing a threat to the DDR itself.

The anxiety felt by NATO's member nations grew substantially as the impasse over Berlin reached its peak, and yet further in July 1961 when a sudden 25% increase in the Soviet defence budget was announced. This came at around the same time as the first major out-of-area exercise by the Soviet Navy off Norway involving eight surface units and submarines. On 25 July, President Kennedy announced that NATO forces 'in-theatre' were to be bolstered under the auspices of Operation *Stair Step*, a large-scale mobilisation of US forces including

A C-124C Globemaster II heading for Europe on one of many flights made by MATS transport aircraft in support of the huge NATO reinforcement.

Reserve and National Guard units that were to deploy to Europe. These moves were hastened when, on 13 August, the East German government constructed a crude concrete wall to divide the Western and Eastern sectors of Berlin, while simultaneously closing 63 of the city's 80 exit points. The USAF provided a number of Tactical Air Command squadrons prior to the arrival of Air National Guard units in October at bases in France, initially with F-84F Thunderstreaks, RF-84F Thunderflashes and F-86H Sabres, and followed by F-104A Starfighters and F-100D Super Sabres. The Military Air Transport Service (MATS) supported the massed deployments with C-97 Stratofreighters and C-124 Globemaster IIs, augmenting those already detached to European bases.

A year prior to these events, France had demanded that the USAF's nuclear-capable aircraft assets be removed from bases on its soil, but six were to house the reinforcements from across the Atlantic, along with Ramstein in Germany and Moron in Spain, which between them took in the F-104s. Of the permanently NATO-assigned USAFE aircraft, the first F-105D Thunderchiefs to serve in Europe had only arrived at Bitburg on 30 June 1961, and alongside the F-100s, were on hand to operate in the fighter-bomber role, had hostilities with the Soviets developed. Already, SAC had placed half of its B-52 Stratofortress force on 50% alert, the 'BUFFs' being at readiness to get airborne within 15 minutes of reports of an impending strike on the US mainland being received. The new concept of airborne command posts was tested, using a modified KC-97 and several KC-135As, and was found to be effective. Fortunately, diplomatic solutions were found and the Berlin Crisis passed off peacefully, although the city remained physically divided by the hastily-erected and defended wall.

The North Atlantic Council strongly condemned the construction of the wall during its ministerial meeting in December 1961, and at the same time announced that diplomatic contacts with the USSR

The first Republic F-105D Thunderchief arrived with USAFE at Bitburg AB, West Germany at the end of June 1961.

were to be resumed to try to further negotiations. East Berlin had to wait, but, as during the Airlift of 1948-49, the Western allies had demonstrated their firm resolve when faced with hostility from the East, underlining still further their commitment to West Berlin and the Federal Republic, as well as to overall European security.

The most serious 'flashpoint' occurred during 1962. Following the Bay of Pigs débâcle of a year before, when a US-supported invasion of Cuba by exiles had failed, the supply of arms by the Soviet Union to Fidel Castro's regime began in earnest. U-2 reconnaissance sorties confirmed the presence on the island of intermediate-range ballistic missiles and Soviet-built Tu-16 *Badger* medium bombers, that could easily reach the US mainland. This placed all USAF assets, including those directly-assigned to NATO in Europe, on the 'front line', as the risk of an attack loomed large. The urgent movement of fighter, bomber and reconnaissance units to Florida

was undertaken, and an arms quarantine imposed on Cuba. The threat of a US invasion proved decisive in the Soviet withdrawal of its weapons, confirmed after an RF-101 mission on 29 October. The arms quarantine was lifted a month later.

With this 'close call' over, NATO forces were stood down from their state of alert. However, one of the significant outcomes of the Cuban crisis was to create a further worry for the Alliance. The naval blockade that had been imposed by the US emphasised to the Soviets that, in spite of the start of sea exercises outside their own waters during the previous year, their naval forces still lacked the strength and expertise in planning a maritime strategy against their primary Cold War 'opponent'. It heralded the start of a long and intensive period of Soviet naval exercises, on a bi-annual basis, which commenced in 1963 and continued with regular transfers of vessels between the Baltic, Northern and Black Sea fleets.

NEW AIRCRAFT

Canadian Armed Forces CF-104 Starfighters

Above: A Coltishall-based RAF Lightning F1A, carrying dummy Firestreak missiles, returning from a training sortie.

Left: This No 92 Squadron Lightning F2A was based (with No 19 Squadron) at RAF Gütersloh in West Germany from 1965.

NEW AIRCRAFT

Right: The introduction of the Dassault Mirage into front-line service with the French Air Force in 1960 was a quantum leap forward.

In June 1960, the RAF gained a 'potentially' supersonic, all-weather interception capability, with the delivery of Fighter Command's first operational English Electric Lightning F1s to No 74 Squadron at RAF Coltishall. With a top speed of Mach 2, it was more than twice as fast in level flight as the Hunter, the fighter it replaced. The Lightning was equipped with a fully-integrated weapons system and had an operational ceiling much higher than anything ever flown before by the Service. Two F1A units from RAF Wattisham, plus a squadron of Javelins, were detached to West Germany towards the end of 1961, as a gesture towards the crisis in Berlin. They soon returned to Britain once the situation returned to 'normal'. However, it took until September 1965 for the 2nd ATAF to receive its first Lightnings, when Nos 19 and 92 Squadrons re-equipped with F2s at RAF Gütersloh.

Also in 1960, the French Air Force began to take delivery of the Dassault Mirage IIIC, the first European-designed aircraft to fly at twice the speed of sound. This was just as large a step forward for the Armée de l'Air as the Lightning was for the RAF. Mirage IIIs initially supplemented the Mystère IVA

in the interceptor role, but offered a far superior air-to-air weapons capability and overall performance. These early aircraft were equipped with rocket motors for use on high-altitude missions (the initial requirement had in fact been for a dual turbojet/rocket-powered interceptor) but these were seldom-used operationally and soon removed.

Although not directly affecting NATO land-based air forces at first, the McDonnell F4H-1 Phantom's entry into service with the US Navy in late 1960 was significant. Re-designated the F-4B in its first production form, the type was first deployed aboard an aircraft carrier, the USS *Enterprise* (the USN's initial nuclear carrier) during 1962. Twelve squadrons of the Atlantic Fleet had been equipped with Phantoms by 1965, along with nine in the Pacific Fleet. Others followed, as hostilities in South-East Asia developed. As a contribution to NATO, the Atlantic Fleet's F-4B units provided air defence cover for US naval forces within the Alliance's area of operation as well as further afield. In particular, numerous fleet deployments to the Mediterranean saw the aircraft regularly taking part in joint operations with NATO's permanent

European-based assets. The Phantom's significance to the Alliance was to become much greater before the decade was over.

Another new naval strike fighter that entered service in the early 1960s was the Royal Navy's Blackburn Buccaneer S1. The nuclear-capable strike aircraft was taken to sea operationally for the first time by No 809 Naval Air Squadron on HMS *Ark Royal* during early 1963. The improved S2 followed in 1965, and the total of Buccaneer squadrons was increased from three to four, embarking upon the carriers *Ark Royal*, *Hermes*, *Victorious* and *Eagle*. They participated in many NATO exercises, often alongside US Navy carrier aircraft. Refuelling training, for example, was undertaken with USN Douglas A-3 Skywarriors for the first time in 1967, demonstrating the development of NATO inter-operability.

The Cuban missile crisis forced the USAF to speed up the modernisation plans for its fighter inventory. Whilst the TFX programme, which later resulted in the F-111, did not produce the intended air defence fighter, it was decided to evaluate the US Navy's Phantom for the role. Twenty-nine were 'borrowed' for a series of trials, and compared with the then-current F-106 Delta Dart, which the new machine comfortably out-performed. For USAF

Above: A Royal Navy Buccaneer of No 800 Naval Air Squadron prepares to launch from the flight deck of HMS *Eagle* during a NATO exercise.

Left: Slow approach for a carrier deck-landing by a Royal Navy Buccaneer S2.

Carrying an underwing refuelling pod, this US Navy EKA-3B Skywarrior was well equipped for anti-radiation and conventional attack.

service, the McDonnell fighter was initially designated as the F-110A Spectre, though this was soon changed to F-4C Phantom. The 12th and 15th Tactical Fighter Wings at MacDill AFB, Florida received the first Phantoms as full series production got under way for the Air Force. Several changes were made to the Phantom for USAF service, most notably the use of Pratt & Whitney J79-15 engines and the AN/APQ-100 radar, which added an enhanced ground attack capability. With American military attention focused away from NATO towards the growing problem in Southeast Asia, it was here that the Phantom received its baptism of fire.

While the RAF and French Armée de l'Air opted for indigenous products in the mid-1960s as their new fighters, Canada and other European NATO countries were involved in what became known as the 'sale of the century' (a phrase which would re-appear in a similar NATO context some years later).

Three of the first production F-104G Starfighters that were assembled by SABCA at Gosselies for the Belgian Air Force.

Left: Having placed the first order for multi-role F-104Gs in November 1958, the Luftwaffe became, by far, the largest operator of the Starfighter in Europe.

A requirement in the late 1950s, shared by the other air forces within the Alliance, for a supersonic, multi-role, nuclear-capable fighter, received a sizeable response from the US aircraft industry, which managed to beat off competition from the Lightning and Mirage III, both of which were also offered. The maximum sales potential for one aircraft would have been up to 2,000 units, a rich reward for the winner.

When the Luftwaffe selected a version of the Lockheed F-104 Starfighter optimised for NATO's multi-role needs in November 1958, the decision was met with some surprise. The F-104 had seen only limited USAF service and was gradually being phased out of front-line use. It had also suffered a high accident rate in its few years of operations. The first batch of 96 Lockheed-built F-104Gs ordered by West Germany was augmented by a contract for 30 two-seat F-104F conversion trainers; while a licence production agreement resulted in another 574 Starfighters being built. Canada was the next Starfighter buyer, ordering 200 single-seat CF-104s

in July 1959, along with 38 two-seat CF-104Ds, to be built by Canadair.

With the Netherlands, Belgium and then Italy ordering Starfighters in 1960-61, arrangements were made with Lockheed for licence production at several European locations. In Germany, the ARGE Süd manufacturing working group comprised Messerschmitt, who undertook final assembly, Dornier, Heinkel and Siebel, while BMW produced the J79 engines. This group manufactured the first Luftwaffe F-104Gs, and subsequently aircraft for the Federal German Navy, the Bundesmarine, who purchased the type in 1963 for commonality, taking ARGE Süd's production to 210 units. A northern manufacturing group, ARGE Nord, included Focke-Wulf and Hamburger Flugzeugbau, with final assembly taking place in the Netherlands, by Fokker at Amsterdam-Schipol. From the 350 F-104s produced here, 255 went to Germany and 95 to the Royal Netherlands Air Force.

Meanwhile, the western production combine took in Belgium's Avions Fairey and SABCA, co-

Visiting the UK in August 1971, this Canadian Armed Forces CF-104 Starfighter was based at Baden Sollingen, West Germany. The CAF had four Wings flying in support of NATO, each with two squadrons of CF-104s.

The Starfighter served with Marinefliegergeschwadern (MFG) 1 and 2, units of the Federal German Navy that were equipped with fighter and reconnaissance versions.

located at Gosselies, plus engine manufacturer Fabrique Nationale in Brussels, who collectively supplied 88 F-104Gs to Germany and 100 to the Belgian Air Force. Construction of F-104s in Italy was led by Fiat, with components coming from Alfa Romeo and Macchi. Fiat supplied 125 aircraft to the Italian Air Force, 50 to Germany and 25 to the Netherlands from its assembly lines at Turin. Underlining just what an enormous undertaking the Starfighter purchase was for NATO, it established an F-104 production co-ordinating centre in Koblenz in 1960 to oversee all four industrial groups.

The Luftwaffe became the first of the new NATO Starfighter operators when Jagdbombergeschwader 31 became operational on the F-104G at Nörvenich in February 1961. 605 of the 700 aircraft ordered by the FRG were used by the Air Force, of which 395 were nuclear-capable fighter bombers, 107 were interceptors and 103 became reconnaissance RF-104Gs. The remaining allocation of 95 went to the

Bundesmarine, again including some recce versions. However, the type's initial NATO service record was far from good, with Germany, the largest operator, suffering a steadily increasing number of accidents, peaking at 28 aircraft lost during 1965. The German press dubbed the F-104 the 'Widow-maker', after the number of fatal accidents reached crisis proportions.

Although there had been problems with the F-104's J79 powerplant's afterburner and other teething troubles, most blame was attached to pilot error for the severe spate of crashes. The training provision for F-104 air- and groundcrew, and a lack of flying hours for German Starfighter pilots, compared with the NATO average, were identified as the prime causes, coupled with the switch from flying in cloudless skies at Luke AFB, Arizona, during initial F-104 conversion training to the much less predictable conditions of Europe, upon joining the Luftwaffe squadrons. The service's chief,

Left: Widely adopted by
NATO air forces, F-104Gs
were supplied to Norway,
and funded under MDAP.

Each air arm received a number of two-seat F-104Ds for pilot conversion and operational training. This example was flown by the Royal Danish Air Force.

Gen. Werner Panitzki, resigned over the problem, describing the purchase of the type as a 'political decision'. His replacement, Lt. Gen. Johannes Steinhoff, a former World War 2 Me262 pilot, implemented new training procedures for the F-104, and measures were taken to improve pilot survivability by fitting Martin Baker ejector seats. Subsequently, German Starfighter losses stabilised at a slightly more moderate rate, similar to the totals of the other new NATO Starfighter operators.

More NATO air arms adopted the F-104, including Denmark, Greece, Norway and Turkey, supplied in most cases through MDAP funding. Despite its initial difficulties, the F-104 became a key element of NATO's military strategy. Canadian operational units equipped with CF-104s were all based in Europe, equipping a maximum of eight squadrons based under four Wings at Baden-Söllingen, Lahr and Zweibrücken during the mid-1960s. Apart from the two reconnaissance squadrons, their main role during the period was nuclear strike. Similarly, the Starfighters of the other NATO air arms had the carriage of the B43 tactical nuclear weapon as their primary role, along with a secondary conventional weapons capability. Five Luftwaffe Jagdbombergeschwadern received F-104Gs, along with two Jagdgeschwadern for interceptor duties, two Aufklärungsgeschwadern for reconnaissance, and the weapons conversion unit. The F-104 was also in the front-line as a maritime strike platform, with two Federal German Navy Marinefliegergeschwadern using both F-104Gs and RF-104Gs.

Belgium's F-104Gs were divided between 1 Wing for air defence, and 10 Wing in the nuclear/conventional strike role, each with two squadrons. Likewise the Royal Danish Air Force operated multi-role aircraft. The Italian F-104Gs were almost equally divided between interceptors and strike aircraft, augmented by a Stormo (wing) of RF-104Gs, and those of the Royal Netherlands Air Force were assigned in equal measure to interceptor and attack duties, together with a single squadron in reconnaissance configuration. Norway was the only nation not to use its F-104s in the strike role, while the small Hellenic Air Force fleet was only used for strike/attack.

Although the Starfighter, in spite of its early shortcomings, had widespread use by the NATO air arms, providing some measure of standardisation, this was not achieved by another project developed specifically to meet an Alliance requirement. This was the NBMR-2 specification for a new long-range maritime patrol aircraft, issued in 1957. It was met by the Breguet Br1150 that was produced by an industrial group that included Belgium's SABCA and SONACA, Italy's Aeritalia, Fokker in the Netherlands and West Germany's Messerschmitt Bolkow-Blohm, in addition to Breguet in France. The prototype took to the air for the first time on 21 October 1961, and the Atlantic, as it was named, entered service five years later. Its initial operators were the French Aéronavale (replacing P-2 Neptunes) and West German Bundesmarine, with deliveries commencing in December 1965. The Netherlands and Italy followed with later orders.

The specific requirements of other NATO nations meant that, like the Fiat G-91, the Atlantic was not destined for widespread adoption. It did not meet the RAF's maritime patrol needs (for which the Hawker Siddeley Nimrod was being developed, to replace the Avro Shackleton) by the time the Breguet machine was ready for service. Other countries either had no requirement for a new maritime patrol type at this stage, or in the case of Norway, were awaiting delivery of the Lockheed P-3 Orion. The Orion had been in US Navy service since August 1962, and P-3A/Bs provided NATO-assigned deployments, particularly to NAS Keflavik in Iceland and Sigonella in Italy.

Although initial plans for its adoption by almost all of the NATO members failed to materialise, the Atlantic project actually came to a successful conclusion. The same cannot be said for the rather more ambitious project, announced in 1961, to provide replacements for both the F-104 and Fiat G-91, with a vertical takeoff and landing (VTOL) strike fighter aircraft. The NATO requirement, designated NBMR-3, was quickly followed by a further brief, the NBMR-4 for a VTOL transport to support the new strike fighter. In Germany, the Entwicklungsring Süd development team was formed by Heinkel, Messerschmitt and Bolkow to

NATO's second specification, for a long-range maritime patrol aircraft, was met by the Breguet Atlantic. It first entered service in 1966 with the French Navy.

Left: The second German
VJ101C VTOL aircraft had
afterburning propulsion
engines that enabled it to
just exceed Mach 1.

Four of the Hawker Kestrel FGA1s that were evaluated by the tripartite (UK, USA and West Germany) trials squadron in 1964.

build a vertical take-off research fighter, the VJ101C. First flown in 1963, it was not developed for operational use as a G-91 successor owing to the limitations of the design. Difficulties ensued with its tilting wingtip-mounted engines, but much valuable research for the actual combat aircraft prototypes on the drawing boards had been gathered.

The Hawker Siddeley P1154, a supersonic development of the Hawker P1127/Kestrel FGA1, was declared winner of the F-104 replacement requirement, from the drawing board. A tripartite evaluation of the Kestrel, involving the UK, USA and West Germany commenced in 1964, providing valuable experience of the British VTOL concept. From the USA, Lockheed submitted various VTOL Starfighter proposals and Dassault continued to champion its Mirage IIIV, which, in January 1965 was the only one of the pair to actually fly. As far as the G-91 replacement went, Germany and Italy, both 'Gina' operators, jointly produced the VAK 191 requirement in 1963, which was met by the Hawker P1127, Focke-Wulf Fw1262, EWR 420 and Fiat G95/4. Of these, the EWR aircraft was a 'refined' VJ101, but it was Focke-Wulf's project which best satisfied the prospective customers and went forward to the advanced development and construction stage. The new VFW company, formed in late 1963, which included Focke-Wulf, was joined by Fiat to undertake this project.

Below: Based on the Focke-Wulf Fw1262, the VAK 191 was built by VFW to meet a joint German and Italian requirement, but did not proceed beyond the three prototype aircraft.

However, plans were soon overtaken by events. NATO decided that forthcoming changes in its battle strategy demanded that aircraft would no longer carry the tactical nuclear strike task, and it was announced in 1965 that neither of the VTOL strike fighters, nor the supporting transport (for which role helicopters were deemed to still be well suited), were required. In spite of this, useful development was carried out for several years afterwards. As far as the transport was concerned, Hawker Siddeley put forward the HS129, and the Dornier Do31E flew in its final prototype form in July 1967, but there was no subsequent civil or military interest. The VAK 191B finally took to the air in late 1971 to begin a research programme for the future Multi-Role Combat Aircraft (MRCA) programme.

The abandonment of the low-level nuclear attack requirement was part of a much wider 'overhaul' of NATO thinking which ensued from lengthy discussions in the early/mid-1960s. The 'tripwire' policy, whereby an attack of any size on an Alliance member would be met with a response of all-out war, was replaced with a new 'flexible response' strategy which would see the reaction by NATO being proportional to the initial degree of aggression. Significantly, this now recognised that a Soviet attack might not now be in the form of an all-out nuclear onslaught, but instead might have

This Boeing EC-135H *Silk Purse* airborne command post was based at RAF Mildenhall from 1965, with the 10th ACCS.

rather more limited aims. Now, the emphasis was to be placed on containing any escalations in a potential armed conflict, rather than aiming at total destruction of the USSR – this could after all have seen the Soviets meting the same out to NATO.

Conventional forces were to assume greater importance within the Alliance, and nuclear weapons were now only to be used if the Alliance's defences were close to collapse. However, the risk of inadequate defence in a time of war, allowing a Warsaw Pact onslaught into West Germany up to the Rhine, meant that a nuclear deterrent would

remain in-theatre, albeit in a somewhat reduced form. Although this was announced to the German government in 1966, the F-104s assigned to the air-to-ground role were not re-tasked for purely conventional tactical strike duties until the new policy was officially adopted in 1971-72.

The 1960s were also a time of structural change within NATO, directly affecting its air arms. It was announced in May 1963 that SACEUR was to have under its command all of the RAF's operational 'V-bombers'. Prior to this, only the Valiant squadrons had been directly NATO-assigned, together with

major metal fatigue concerns. At this stage, there was still a degree of uncertainty regarding the RAF's contribution to NATO's strategic deterrent. Some 60 Douglas Thor intermediate-range ballistic missiles provided by the USA in 1958 were by now being retired owing to the difficulty of their operation, and the shootdown of Gary Powers' U-2 illustrated the danger posed by Soviet SAMs to any flights over their territory. Air-launched stand-off nuclear weapons had in the meantime been required by the RAF for use by the 'V-force', and it had been announced in 1960 that the Avro Blue Steel stand-off weapon was to be replaced by the Douglas Skybolt, again provided by the USA, with its much greater range. However, when the latter weapon was cancelled by President Kennedy in 1962, there was no option but to return to using Blue Steel, and await the delivery of the submarine-launched Polaris system for the Royal Navy who would now have to assume the strategic nuclear role.

Following John F. Kennedy's assassination in November 1963, the succeeding President Lyndon Johnson reaffirmed the United States' position, stating in a message to the North Atlantic Council that his nation pledged 'steadfast resolve' to NATO. This had been demonstrated earlier in 1963, when USAF C-130 Hercules and other transports – supported by fighter-bombers, reconnaissance assets and tankers – airlifted 14,893 troops of the 2nd Armored Division from Bergstrom AFB, Texas to airfields in France and Germany, in a graphic illustration of the very rapid reinforcement available in the event of any hostilities developing.

A new permanent USAF asset assigned to NATO in Europe began operations in 1965, when the *Silk Purse* control group and its Boeing EC-135H airborne command posts started operating with the 10th Airborne Command and Control Squadron at RAF Mildenhall. In the same year an era ended, when the final SAC B-47 Stratojets on *Reflex Action* alert based at Upper Heyford and Brize Norton in the UK, were flown back to the USA. Now, for the first time since 1947 (and the formation of the USAF), there was no constant rotational presence by the Command in Britain. Periodic visits were made by B-52s, but on a much more occasional basis, usually to take part in exercises.

On the plus side, the first RF-4C Phantom IIs

the US Navy's Polaris nuclear submarines. Coincidentally, 1963 also saw the signing of the Moscow Treaty by the UK, USA and USSR, which banned nuclear tests in the atmosphere, outer space and under water. The involvement of the Soviet Union in the talks marked the start of a period of relative détente between the superpowers, although underlying tensions still ran high on specific issues.

The number of RAF Bomber Command squadrons operating Valiants, Victors or Vulcans reached its peak in 1963 at 22, although the entire Valiant force was to be retired in 1965 owing to

arrived with USAFE's 10th Tactical Reconnaissance Wing at RAF Alconbury in May 1965, replacing the elderly RB-66 Destroyers. Their arrival started a new chapter for NATO as these were the first Phantoms to be based in Europe. Reconnaissance units based in France were subsequently re-equipped. Towards the end of the year, the F-101s of the 81st Tactical Fighter Wing at RAF Bentwaters began to depart, heralding their replacement by F-4C Phantoms in the fighter role. The last Voodoos left during April 1966, and soon afterwards more capable F-4Ds superseded the earlier machines with the 81st TFW.

It was not long, however, before the effects of the Vietnam conflict began to tell somewhat on the USAF presence in Europe. Two Wings based in Germany relinquished their F-105 Thunderchiefs to go as attrition replacements, B-66Bs were moved from France to Southeast Asia, and the C-130s of Military Airlift Command which had become such familiar sights at all USAFE bases gave up their transport tasking to C-97G Stratofreighters and C-121 Constellations drawn from Air National Guard units. Although these were not major changes, they illustrate the impact that the war had on all aspects of the USAF worldwide, including its NATO commitments.

As a result of these moves, the 36th Tactical Fighter Wing at Bitburg AB, West Germany, received F-4D Phantoms for the first time in 1966, in place of urgently-required F-105s. Another new operator of the McDonnell fighter in the same year was the Hahn-based 50th TFW, replacing F-100 Super Sabres. The 49th TFW based at Spangdahlem converted from the F-105 to the F-4D in 1967, but then moved back to Holloman AFB, New Mexico. However, as part of a 'dual-basing' concept, they remained under the aegis of NATO, with squadrons returning regularly to West Germany over the next five years, during *Reforger* rapid deployment exercises. These exercises, which commenced in the

Top: The first McDonnell Douglas Phantoms seen in Europe were grey/white RF-4Cs, that replaced the elderly RB-66 Destroyers at RAF Alconbury in May 1965.

Left: Displaying the base code AR on its tail, this camouflaged 32nd Tactical Reconnaissance Squadron RF-4C is seen taking off from Alconbury.

A C-130E Hercules, in the camouflage scheme that was adopted for operations in Southeast Asia, on TDY with the 317th Troop Carrier Wing at RAF Mildenhall.

late 1960s, brought ever closer ties between US-based forces and those in Europe, a very important move in the light of the continuing Cold War.

While Germany remained very much a focus of East-West tension in Europe (as re-affirmed in May 1965 by a North Atlantic Council declaration, which stated that the division of Germany would maintain the unsettled nature of the situation), it was France which was to cause the next major change in NATO. Under President de Gaulle, the nation had become an increasingly independent voice within the Alliance, as evidenced by its leader's refusal to sign the nuclear test ban document under the Moscow Treaty. Added to this was de Gaulle's belief that, in reality, the USA would not meet a strike on Western Europe with the immediate nuclear response that was fundamental to NATO policy. This disenchantment led the French President to announce on 9 September 1965 that his country would end its military integration in NATO within four years, a decision that would have a significant effect on the Alliance over a long period.

This began in earnest in March 1966, when President de Gaulle officially communicated his intentions to his opposite number in the USA, Lyndon Johnson. Three days after this, on 10 March, other NATO members were informed that the military forces and headquarters were to be removed from France, a process which, it had been declared, would have to be complete by 1 April 1967. The problems this presented were raised during a Ministerial Session of the North Atlantic Council in Brussels. On 21 June, the announcement was made that SHAPE (which had previously been based at Rocquencourt near Paris) would be moved to Belgium, the site at Casteau near Mons being selected in September. Other important NATO organisations that were forced to find new homes outside of France included the Defense College, that moved to Rome; Allied Forces Central Europe (AFCENT) moved to Brunssum in the Netherlands and, most significantly, NATO Headquarters itself which relocated from Paris to Brussels. Shortly afterwards, in the interests of centralisation, the Alliance's Military Committee left Washington, DC for the Belgian capital.

In terms of air power assets, it was the USAF which was most affected by the French withdrawal from NATO's military structures. Despite the enforced departure of its nuclear-capable fighter-bombers in 1960, a number of flying units, and of course personnel, remained. The Third Air Force in the UK expanded as a result – C-130 Hercules on TDY with the 317th Troop Carrier (later Tactical Airlift) Wing changed the location of their deployments to RAF Mildenhall, Suffolk, which began a long residence for C-130s in East Anglia. RF-4Cs of the 32nd Tactical Reconnaissance Squadron arrived at RAF Alconbury, and the 66th TRW RF-101Cs found a new home at RAF Upper

Heyford. Later, the Vietnam conflict demanded that some of the C-130s left Europe for the Southeast Asian theatre, and were replaced at Mildenhall by Air Force Reserve C-124 Globemaster IIs, that stayed until 1969. Canada was the only other country that had to move aircraft out of France, bolstering the German-based units with further CF-104 Starfighters in the fighter/attack and recce roles.

1967 saw the now re-located NATO installations being opened, beginning on 18 January with the Defense College in Rome, followed by SHAPE at Casteau, AFCENT at Brunssum and finally NATO Headquarters in Brussels on 16 October. Following publication of the Harmel Report on the Future Tasks of the Alliance, it was announced in December 1967 that the Defence Planning Committee was to adopt the Flexible Response concept, and the establishment of a Standing Naval Force Atlantic (STANAVFORLANT) was authorised. The new command was inaugurated in January 1968 at HMS *Osprey*, the Royal Navy's Portland base. This came at a particularly appropriate time as

Soviet naval activity was increasing rapidly. The Arab-Israeli Six Day War of 1967 produced numerous USSR maritime deployments and cruises, and later in 1968 a very large exercise in the Norwegian Sea involved many surface units and submarines with maritime reconnaissance sorties flown by Tupolev Tu-95 *Bears* and Tu-16 *Badgers* in support. These aircraft, from both the Soviet Air Force's Long-Range Aviation and Soviet Naval Aviation, along with the latter's Ilyushin Il-20 *Coots* and later Il-38 *Mays*, probed the northern NATO air defence region on fairly regular occasions during their lengthy ELINT-gathering and reconnaissance missions.

In May 1968, the Defence Planning Committee again stated that a balance of forces between NATO and the Warsaw Pact states was desirable, and to that end a number of goals were set which were to be met by the Alliance by 1973. In addition, it was agreed that an anti-ballistic missile system was not required in Europe. However, a new period of East-West tension started soon afterwards with the

An intelligence gathering Tupolev Tu-95 *Bear* from Soviet Naval Aviation photographed shadowing a NATO exercise in the North Sea.

Although funded under MDAP as a lightweight fighter for NATO, the CAF assigned its Canadair-built CF-5s to the North American Air Defence System.

Below: Northrop F-5A and two-seat F-5B of the Royal Norwegian Air Force – 108 of the type were supplied to this air arm from 1966.

invasion of Czechoslovakia by troops from several Warsaw Pact states (the USSR, Bulgaria, East Germany, Hungary and Poland) on 20-21 August 1968. An emergency meeting of the North Atlantic Council was held, and as the situation continued to develop through the rest of the year with the announcement that Soviet troops would be 'temporarily' stationed in the country, the Council issued a warning to the USSR, denouncing the invasion as being 'contrary to the basic principles of the United Nations Charter'. Again, a 'temporary measure' on the part of the Soviets would prove to be rather more permanent.

A long-running aircraft development programme for NATO, begun as far back as 1954 by the US government in order to supply a cheap, lightweight fighter via the MDAP, was by now bearing operational fruit, as in 1966 the Royal Norwegian Air Force took delivery of its first Northrop F-5 out of 108 ordered. This was made up of 78 single-seat F-5As, 14 two-seater F-5Bs and 15 reconnaissance RF-5As. Six KNL squadrons used the Freedom Fighter during the early 1970s. Some 240 Canadair-built CF-5s (locally designated CF-116s) were also being produced, assigned upon service entry to NORAD, and these light fighter-bombers were

Above left: The Belgian
Air Force replaced its F-84
Thunderstreaks with over
100 Dassault Mirage Vs,
including this VBR
reconnaissance version.

followed off the production line by the equivalent NF-5A/Bs for the Royal Netherlands Air Force, which began arriving in KLu squadrons during 1969. Three were to become operational, Nos 314 (at Eindhoven), 315 (based at Twenthe) and 316 (at Gilze Rijen). The Dutch aircraft were purchased to replace the KLu's final F-84 Thunderstreaks, but the Belgian Air Force selected Dassault Mirage Vs for this purpose. The 63 attack variants, designated VBAs, were augmented by 27 recce VBRs and 16 two-seat VBD conversion trainers. They went to Florennes-based 2 Wing and 3 Wing at Liège/ Bierset, beginning in June 1970.

Another addition to NATO's front-line inventory at around this time was the Italian Air Force's F-104S Starfighter, a version developed especially for their all-weather interceptor requirement. The 'S' in the designation indicated that the new variant, the last of the famous Starfighter line to be built new, was capable of carrying the AIM-7E Sparrow AAM amongst an increased overall array of stores. After the initial development and pre-production phases were undertaken in the USA, all the F-104Ss received by the AMI from 1969 were built in Italy by

Fiat (later Aeritalia) while Selenia supplied the Sparrow missiles, and FIAR the radars. The Turkish Air Force subsequently ordered 40 F-104S versions, used by 9 Ana Jet Us based at Balikesir.

Meanwhile, the Royal Danish Air Force was beginning to modernise its attack capability, replacing part of its long-serving F-100 Super Sabre fleet. The aircraft chosen, uniquely for a NATO member country, was the Saab 35 Draken, and three variants were to be received: 20 A35XD strike derivatives, another 20 tactical recce S35XDs, and finally six two-seat Sk35XD conversion trainers (five more of the latter being added upon the RDAF's retirement of the Lockheed T-33 in 1976). Two former Super Sabre units changed to the Draken, Eskadrilles 725 and 729 – both based at Karup - leaving the two squadrons at Skyrdstrup to soldier on with the veteran North American design for some time yet.

In the final years of the decade, the Royal Air Force embarked upon a major re-equipment programme amongst a number of its front-line units, and changes of tasking. The obsolete maritime reconnaissance version of the Avro

An F-84 Thunderstreak
formating with a Northrop
NF-5B and a Soesterburg-
based USAFE Phantom.
All came under the day-to-
day control of the Royal
Netherlands Air Force.

Left: One of six two-seat Saab Drakens that replaced T-33s for conversion and operational training with the Royal Danish Air Force.

Above: It was not until the end of 1969 that the RAF began to replace its Avro Shackletons with the new HS Nimrod MR1 maritime patrol aircraft, developed from the Comet airliner.

Shackleton, which had first flown in 1949 and been operational since 1951, began to be replaced by the Hawker Siddeley Nimrod MR1 from late 1969. The new type became the world's first land-based, all-jet aircraft in the role. Shortly after its introduction, the first operational sortie was undertaken by a Nimrod, when an aircraft from RAF St Mawgan was successfully diverted to locate and follow a small force of Soviet ships 200 miles south-west of Land's End, a task repeated many times since. In September 1970, Nimrod MR1s participated in their first NATO manoeuvres, as part of Exercise *Northern Wedding*.

The establishment of RAF Strike Command in April 1968 brought the service's bomber, fighter and, later, maritime reconnaissance assets under a single command, rather than operating under separate

organisations. At the same time, the decision was taken to remove the UK's nuclear deterrent responsibility within NATO from Strike Command's Vulcans and Victors, and transfer it to the Royal Navy's Polaris submarines. A tactical nuclear and increased conventional role was thereby assumed by the Vulcans, while the Victor aircraft were converted for strategic reconnaissance and air-to-air refuelling duties. Meanwhile, the Canberra B(I)8s based in Germany now provided the RAF's only tactical bombing element assigned to NATO. These changes followed a number of cancellations of orders for the RAF during the mid-late 1960s, headed by the BAC TSR2 which was to have replaced the Canberra, the supersonic Hawker Siddeley P1154 V/STOL fighter and the HS681 tactical jet transport. Following on from these, a contract to purchase General Dynamics F-111s to supersede the Canberra was also shelved. In lieu of the above further new aircraft were added to the RAF's NATO-assigned inventory.

The first Rolls-Royce Spey-engined McDonnell Douglas F-4M Phantom FGR2s arrived in July 1968 with No 228 Operational Conversion Unit at RAF Coningsby. The first operational strike squadron, No 6, formed the following May and No 43 Squadron, the initial RAF air defence unit to fly F-4s, converted onto the Phantom FG1 in September. The Royal Navy's F-4K Phantom FG1s had by now begun to be allocated to No 892 Naval Air Squadron, superseding the de Havilland Sea Vixen FAW2 as the air arm's primary strike fighter.

Above: An RAF Vulcan B2 of No 27 Squadron carrying a Blue Steel stand-off weapon, a substitute for the Douglas Skybolt ordered by the British government that had been cancelled by the US President.

Left: Canberra B(I)8s were the RAF's only tactical bombers assigned to NATO until Phantom FGR2s came into service as an interim measure in 1970.

Right: A Rolls-Royce Spey-powered F-4M Phantom of No 43 Squadron, the first RAF unit to operate the air defence version, that became operational at RAF Leuchars at the end of 1969.

F-4K Phantom FG1s of No
892 Naval Air Squadron,
Fleet Air Arm following a
joint exercise with the US
Navy carrier *Saratoga* in
the Mediterranean.

However, only HMS *Ark Royal* was now left in use as the sole RN carrier suitable for Phantom operations, and so half of the FG1s were transferred to the RAF for air defence. This reduction in the RN carrier force had also seen major cuts in the Buccaneer S2 inventory, previously flown by four squadrons, of which No 809 NAS was that which detached to *Ark Royal*. Its Phantoms and Buccaneers were regular participants in NATO exercises throughout the 1970s.

RAF Germany began to gain Phantoms in June 1970, soon equipping Nos II(AC), 14, 17 and 31 Squadrons – the former at Laarbrüch had previously flown Hunter FR10s, with the other three forming a wing at Brüggen that was formerly a Canberra B(I)8 operator. Another new asset was added to RAF Strike Command during October 1969, as No 12 Squadron at RAF Honington received its first Hawker Siddeley Buccaneer S2As, the new type (for the RAF at least) having a nuclear capability as well as the capacity to carry a variety of conventional stores in its low-level strike role. Surplus Royal Navy examples had been transferred to the RAF, augmented by new-build machines. Looking ahead, the agreement signed in May 1969 between the UK, West Germany and Italy to develop the Multi-Role Combat Aircraft (MRCA) was a very important step forward for the air arms of all three countries.

Right: A line-up of No 20 Squadron Harrier GR1s at RAF Wildenrath, before the RAF Germany V/STOL squadrons (Nos 3 and 4 Squadrons) moved to RAF Gütersloh.

A significant event for the RAF and its contribution to NATO during this period was the entry into service in July 1969 of the world's first operational fixed-wing V/STOL aircraft, the Hawker Siddeley Harrier GR1, with No 1 Squadron at RAF Wittering. Optimised for the close battlefield support role, the revolutionary Harrier could be operated from small unprepared strips and clearings, and other dispersed sites. In this and other respects the revolutionary V/STOL aircraft was ideally suited to the new concepts of containment and battlefield support in NATO's European theatre.

To this end, while No 1 Squadron had as its primary tasking the reinforcement of the Alliance's flanks – particularly to the North and South – the Harrier units operating in West Germany were deployed as close as possible to the Eastern border, with Nos 3 and 4 Squadrons (following the early disbandment of No 20) moving from their initial base at Wildenrath to a new home at RAF Gütersloh in 1970, to be nearer to the potential front line.

The revolutionary Hawker Siddeley Harrier GR1 first entered service with No 1 Squadron at RAF Wittering in July 1969.

NEW CHALLENGES

US Air Force General Dynamics F-111F

NEW CHALLENGES

With a distinctive shark's mouth marking, this F-4E Phantom was operated by the 86th Tactical Fighter Wing at RAF Bentwaters, when photographed.

The new decade opened on a positive note. The Non-Proliferation Treaty on Nuclear Weapons, that had been tabled at the Geneva Disarmament Conference two years previously, was brought into effect on 5 March 1970. Just over a month later, negotiations opened in Vienna on the Strategic Arms Limitation Treaty (SALT), and a second session followed in Helsinki during November. In other important moves towards détente, a formal declaration was made by NATO foreign ministers in December 1969 regarding East-West relations. This laid out plans for future negotiations, including a European security conference, aimed at discussing a wide range of issues and in particular the status of Berlin.

Several of these issues were progressed in the latter half of 1970. Federal German Chancellor Willy Brandt (a former Mayor of West Berlin) was very much at the forefront of the negotiations. His policy of 'Ostpolitik' – promoting discussion with the East in relation to the DDR, and wider European security issues – was fruitful, despite maintaining the West's firm position on Berlin. Following the decision to open talks between the two Germanies in January, the USSR agreed to discuss the future of Berlin. The signing in Moscow of a Non-Aggression Treaty between West Germany and the Soviets in August 1970, and then a similar move with Poland, were positive steps forward. In June 1972, the Quadripartite Agreement on Berlin was finally signed by the USA, UK, West Germany and USSR, the latter recognising the city's status but not allowing any further concessions.

Continuing arms control talks led to the signing of the SALT agreement by US President Richard Nixon and the Soviet leader Leonid Brezhnev, in Moscow during May 1972. This set new limits on ballistic missile deployments and offensive capability, but the new mood of optimism which ensued was premature. Final agreement on its exact terms was all but impossible to reach – the USSR wanted specific controls on the USA's bomber, cruise and ballistic missile development, while American attention was focused on Soviet ICBMs. When the Mutual Balanced Force Reduction (MBFR) talks resumed in 1971, NATO hoped to bring about reductions in Warsaw Pact military strength. These would have to be much larger than those required of NATO to achieve a more equitable balance. It came as no surprise that the Soviets were unwilling to consider this.

The USAF's F-4 Phantom force in Europe was appreciably strengthened in the 1970s. USAFE's 32nd Tactical Fighter Squadron at Soesterberg in The Netherlands was the first to be equipped with the improved F-4E for the air defence role. It was soon joined by one of the 36th TFW's component squadrons at Bitburg, followed by one of the Hahn-based 50th TFW squadrons, prior to the whole of the 401st TFW at Torrejon AB, Spain receiving the fighter. In 1973, a number of important equipment changes were made in USAFE, the most significant affecting Spangdahlem's 52nd TFW. The Wing relinquished its last B-66 Destroyers, and worked up to full operations with F-4C Phantoms equipped to detect, locate and then eliminate enemy radar sites.

Taxying for take-off, a pair of Spangdahlem-based F-4E Phantoms carry external fuel tanks for a long flight.

Although these *Wild Weasel* Phantoms only had 'interim' systems, they were a major step forward and provided invaluable operational experience, prior to the definitive F-4 *Weasels* arriving.

Another very important new type was delivered to USAFE in 1970, following delays and teething troubles with the initial variants. The first General Dynamics F-111A had arrived with the 474th TFW at Nellis AFB in October 1967, followed two years later by the FB-111A for SAC. However, technical problems delayed its effective use, in spite of an early combat evaluation deployment to Vietnam. These technical and operational difficulties had been ironed out by the time the first F-111Es began to arrive at RAF Upper Heyford in September 1970 for the based 20th TFW, where they replaced elderly F-100 Super Sabres. The new variable-geometry F-111s, with their greater payload, range and speed, carrying either conventional or nuclear weapons

soon gave NATO one of its principal strike/attack assets. The 'Aardvark', as it was nicknamed, would have spearheaded NATO missions deep into Soviet territory had the Cold War burst into hostile action.

The withdrawal of the F-100 from USAFE was finally completed in 1972, when the 48th TFW at RAF Lakenheath replaced its Super Sabres with

Above: The last of the 20th TFW's F-100 Super Sabres departed from RAF Upper Heyford with the arrival of General Dynamics F-111Es, while Phantoms (below) replaced most other frontline types in USAFE.

Right: Demonstrating their swing-wing capability, a trio of USAF F-111s show the fully-swept, half-swept and fully-forward wing positions while flying line-astern.

F-4D Phantoms. However, the worsening situation in Southeast Asia reduced the USAF's commitment to NATO, with a resulting shortfall of aircraft. Further north, the 57th Fighter Interceptor Squadron at NAS Keflavik, Iceland took on F-4Cs to replace its ageing F-102 Delta Daggers. In so doing it became one of the few US Air Defense Command units to operate Phantoms.

As the F-4 became almost standard USAFE front-line equipment, and comprised a major part of the RAF's strike inventory, it was also selected by the Federal German Air Force. The Luftwaffe needed the fighter to enhance its capabilities between the ageing F-104 Starfighter and introduction of the new Panavia MRCA (later named Tornado). Initially, an order was placed for 42 RF-4E Phantoms to replace the RF-104Gs with the Luftwaffe's two tactical reconnaissance wings. The first deliveries were made in 1971 to Aufklärungsgeschwader (AKG) 51 at Bremgarten, followed by Leck-based AKG-52. The RF-4s were flown unarmed, and incorporated much-improved sensor systems compared with those carried by the RF-104s.

When the MRCA's in-service date was delayed well beyond the originally-intended 1975, West Germany elected not to procure the interceptor version and chose to purchase the single-seat F-4F Phantom instead. Optimised for the Luftwaffe, the F-4F had a simplified radar, and substantial production of components was undertaken by the German aerospace industry (including MTU, who licence-built its J79 turbojets, and MBB). Initial deliveries were made to the historic 'Richthofen' Jagdgeschwader 71 at Wittmundhaven in March 1974, and F-4Fs replaced the service's last air defence F-104s (with JG-74, based at Neuberg) in May 1976, by which time two attack-tasked Jagdbombergeschwadern had also received the type. Although JBG-35 phased out its Fiat G-91R/3s in favour of Phantoms and JBG-36 relinquished its F-104s, three units retained the latter type, by now transferred purely to conventional strike as NATO reduced its nuclear capabilities.

The Fiat G-91's service career was not over, as the first aircraft designed specifically to a NATO requirement back in the early 1950s continued to be used by the West German, Italian and Portuguese Air Forces. The Luftwaffe relinquished all of its

As an interim measure between the retirement of its F-104s and delivery of new Tornados, the Luftwaffe acquired Phantoms, starting with 42 RF-4Es (illustrated above) in 1971.

The Luftwaffe passed on many of its G-91Rs and two-seat G-91Ts (right) to the Portuguese Air Force when they were replaced by Phantoms.

G-91R/3s in the attack role by the mid-1980s, but a number of G-91Ts remained on strength with the civilian contractor Condor Flugdienst to provide target facilities. In addition, the twin afterburning J85-engined G-91Y ordered by the Italian Air Force began to reach squadron service in 1970, having been developed specifically for this air arm.

At the beginning of 1974, the RAF started to replace its Phantom FGR2s in the strike role with SEPECAT Jaguar GR1s. The F-4s were transferred to air defence squadrons based at Wildenrath, Germany and Wattisham, Coningsby and Leuchars in the UK. Jaguars entered service with No 54 Squadron, which was soon joined by Nos 6 and 41 Squadrons to form the Coltishall Wing. In Germany the new aircraft replaced Phantoms with Nos 2, 14, 17, 20 and 31 Squadrons. No 41 Squadron at Coltishall and No 2 Squadron at Laarbruch had the specialised fighter reconnaissance role, operating recce-configured aircraft. The Anglo-French Jaguar was a much more capable aircraft than the Phantom with its advanced target-seeking and precision strike

A twin-engined Fiat G-91Y, a version of the 'Gina' that entered service with the Italian Air Force in 1970 and remained on front-line strength for nearly 30 years.

In 1974, Jaguars started to
replace Phantoms with RAF
strike squadrons in the UK
(No 6 Squadron shown) and
in Germany, the F-4s moving
on to air defence duties.

capabilities, and provision for all-weather operations.

No 1 Squadron's Harrier GR1s were hard at work in the early 1970s on exercises, in preparation for its wartime role of supporting NATO forces on the Alliance's flanks. The squadron's first overseas visit was to RAF Akrotiri, Cyprus in March 1970 followed later by a deployment to Bardufoss in Norway. A detachment to HMS *Ark Royal* during 1971 highlighted another side of the Harrier's operational versatility. Nos 3 and 4 Squadrons, based in Germany, began to evaluate the forward-location concept that would see their aircraft deploy from Gütersloh to six 'field' sites along with the necessary support equipment and personnel. Rapid, fairly short-range sorties were then flown, as

demonstrated to NATO in 1974 during Exercise *Big Tee*, when more than ten sorties per aircraft were successfully flown each day. Apart from their primary role in support of the British Army, the Gütersloh Harriers could also have been tasked with backing-up Belgian or West German ground forces, and exercises were carried out to practice this. The only major change to RAF Harrier operations during the 1970s concerned the introduction of the improved GR3, that entered service from 1976. It had new laser range-finding and target-seeking equipment in a re-shaped nose, and improved recce capability, which was a particular responsibility of No 4 Squadron.

NATO concern in the late 1970s centred on the

No 3 Squadron based at RAF Gütersloh (with No 4 Squadron) received the improved Harrier GR3, with its extended 'laser' nose, in 1976.

Above: When the MiG-25 Foxbat first appeared in service during 1973, it caused great concern to NATO, as the West had nothing to match the Russian fighter's speed.

Above right: A pair of Czechoslovak Air Force Sukhoi Su-22M Fitter-Ks, the final version of the successful swing-wing attack fighter.

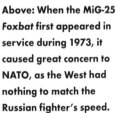

Left: The MiG-23 served widely with the Soviet air arms and Warsaw Pact forces, primarily in the ground-attack version, or the two-seat operational trainer (illustrated).

continuing expansion of the Warsaw Pact's armed forces, and their apparent improved capabilities. This turned the spotlight very much on the efforts of the Organisation to maintain the balance of power. By this time, the MiG-21 *Fishbed* had been still further developed, the -21bis arriving in service in 1972, supplementing earlier MiG-21F-13s, -21PFs/PFMs and -21MFs in Bulgaria, East Germany, Hungary, Poland, Romania and the USSR. At the same time, Soviet Frontal Aviation started to receive the MiG-23M *Flogger* by 1975. This variable-geometry design was capable of operating both as an air superiority fighter and a ground attack aircraft. It was soon replaced in production by the MiG-23ML, which incorporated numerous weapons system and airframe enhancements. *Floggers* went on to serve not just with Frontal Aviation and the PVO air defence regiments, but also in Bulgaria, Czechoslovakia, East Germany, Hungary, Poland and Romania. Most of these air arms also received the dedicated ground-attack variant, the MiG-23BN.

The Soviet PVO's most numerous interceptor was still the Sukhoi Su-15 *Flagon*, which again had been progressively improved during its long service career with the addition of new weapons options and more powerful engines. Far more worrying to

NATO, however, was the appearance of the MiG-25 *Foxbat* from 1973. Capable of reaching Mach 3, the fighter incorporated a look-down, shoot-down radar and was further improved with a systems upgrade in the late 1970s, which helped to counter problems which, at first, had somewhat emasculated this formidable machine. At the time of its service début, the *Foxbat* was believed to be in advance of its then-current NATO counterparts, but subsequent information has shown this to have been a false premise. It was true from the point of view of performance potential but not when its operational capabilities were put to the test.

In updating the Su-7 *Fitter-A*, the Sukhoi Design Bureau gave this already robust and well-performing ground attack aircraft an increased range and better 'off-airfield' operability with, helped by its variable-geometry wing configuration. This second-generation Su-17 *Fitter-C* arrived with Frontal Aviation in the late 1960s, and was followed from 1974 by the Su-17M *Fitter-D* with better avionics and aerodynamics, and the more versatile Su-22M-3 *Fitter-G*, with new weapons options and greater fuel capacity. The latter was sold as a replacement for earlier versions to Hungary, while the Czechoslovak, East German, Polish and Soviet Air Forces all flew the ultimate Su-22M-4K *Fitter-K*, the

After the cancellation of
the Rockwell B-1A in 1977,
the B-52 Stratofortress
bore the weight of NATO's
long-range bomber force,
supported by RAF Vulcans.

best-performing of this long-running Sukhoi family.

Yet another completely new Sukhoi type went into service with Russian Frontal Aviation in 1974. The Sukhoi Su-24 *Fencer* was designed as a supersonic, all-weather precision attack aircraft, with additional photo-reconnaissance and air-to-air combat roles. Its avionics were, for the first time in a Soviet combat aircraft, fully integrated with the weapons system.

In Russian Long-Range Aviation, the Tu-22 *Blinder* fleet had been gradually built up through the 1960s, after service entry early in the decade, although the *Bear* and *Badger* were still numerically very much the mainstays. The Myasishchev M-4 *Bison* was slowly retired from its bombing role, but continued in service as an air-to-air refuelling tanker. The *Bear* was converted to carry stand-off missiles, with the Tu-95K-22 mounting the latest Kh-22 (AS-4) missiles, and equipped with new avionics. In service with Soviet Naval Aviation forces, the Tu-95RT became a familiar sight to NATO interceptor crews around the coast of Europe and as far as the Eastern seaboard of the USA, as the Soviets flew long-range reconnaissance missions. It was followed by the new production Tu-142, the first of the dedicated maritime *Bear-Fs*. The type was given new weapons bays and the latest maritime reconnaissance systems as well as detailed equipment upgrades.

Towards the end of the 1970s, the Tu-22M *Backfire* was added to the Air Force Long-Range Aviation's inventory, making the biggest advance yet in the USSR's strategic attack capabilities. It was much more than a variable-geometry *Blinder*, having exceptional unrefuelled range and genuine Mach 2 performance at altitude, while also being capable of high-speed, low-level penetration sorties. In the West, development of the USAF's comparable Rockwell B-1A was being affected by funding cuts. The B-1's planned production was deferred, before being cancelled by President Carter in 1977 in favour of greater cruise missile procurement. This left the B-52 Stratofortress at the vanguard of NATO's strategic nuclear bomber force, supported by the RAF's Vulcans, while the Soviets now had a very large fleet of *Bears*, together with a growing number of next generation *Backfires*.

The Tu-22M became the focus of controversy in the SALT II talks, at a summit meeting between US President Gerald Ford and Soviet leader Brezhnev, in Vladivostok during November 1974. One of the stumbling blocks which brought about the failure of the summit was the fact that the Soviet leader would not include limitation of the Tu-22M force under SALT II, adding to what was viewed as an imbalance in favour of the USSR in terms of strategic weapons, and reported violations of SALT I by the Soviets. When coupled with Moscow's support for Egypt and Syria (including arms shipments) after their October 1973 attack on (US-backed) Israel, and domestic concerns dominating the American political scene at the time surrounding President Nixon and the Watergate affair, this was not a good period for East-West relations. The failure of so many moves towards détente started to create a degree of resignation to the *status quo* amongst the West European governments, which fed a growing gulf between US policy and those of its NATO allies. Matters were not helped by the 1973 oil crisis and its longer-term effects, particularly the onset of an international recession.

Back on the NATO-WarPac 'battlefield', by the mid-1970s, the USSR had the world's most formidable battlefield attack helicopter in service. The first Mil Mi-24 *Hinds* arrived with the Soviet Army forces in East Germany during 1973. Before too long, the new Mi-24D derivative with its 12.7mm gun, new missile guidance systems and revised cockpit canopy had followed on and become standard equipment. At sea, the USSR was making notable progress – 1976 seeing trials of the Soviet Navy's new small aircraft carrier, the *Kiev*, and the aircraft which provided its offensive capability, the V/STOL Yak-38 *Forger*. Although it had been conceived specifically to operate from this latest class of vessel, the aircraft's attack capability proved to be limited by its relatively small payload. From the outset, the *Forger* had a high accident rate and failed to achieve the success of the RAF's Harrier and later, the Royal Navy's Sea Harrier. However, the fact that the Soviets now possessed a carrier-based attack force with potential for further development, was of great concern to Western strategists, and a major psychological boost to the USSR. Three further *Kiev*-class vessels were in fact built, the *Baku*, *Novorossiisk* and *Minsk*, all equipped with

When the McDonnell Douglas F-15A Eagle entered service with the 36th TFW at Bitburg in 1977, it marked a major step forward in USAFE's air defence capability, as its performance exceeded that of the Soviet MiG-25.

Yak-38s and anti-submarine Kamov Ka-25 *Hormone* helicopters.

The newly appointed US Secretary of Defense, James Schlesinger, soon helped to place defence issues back at the head of the international agenda. He advocated a new awareness towards the Soviet threat, especially its impressive build-up of nuclear forces and air power, but combined with caution and forward thinking. Among Schlesinger's aims was the retention of a variety of nuclear and conventional force options in the US arsenal to respond appropriately to a potential threat, while avoiding a new arms race between the superpowers. In addition, he wanted US defence spending raised and force levels in Europe maintained. While its overall front-line strength remained below those of the Warsaw Pact, NATO was still superior in terms of the capabilities of these forces, especially its air power and more sophisticated command and control network. In addition, further support from all three US services remained available, to be called upon in times of crisis. The rapid trans-Atlantic deployment of these reserves was regularly practised with major *Reforger* and smaller scale exercises.

The first flights of a number of significant new combat aircraft in the mid-1970s indicated that the West had to an extent anticipated the new technology that the Soviets were already bringing into service. In January 1974, the prototype General Dynamics YF-16 made its maiden flight, followed in June by its counterpart in the USAF's Lightweight Tactical Fighter (later Air Combat Fighter) programme, the Northrop YF-17. A competitive fly-off between the pair resulted in selection of the F-16 in January 1975. In Europe, initial flight-testing of the Panavia Multi-Role Combat Aircraft (MRCA) began in April 1974. It was re-named Tornado a month later and prototypes were airborne in Germany, Italy and the UK by the end of the following year.

Two F-15As of the 32nd TFS that replaced Phantoms at Soesterburg, the squadron's Netherlands base, in the autumn of 1978.

Although these aircraft were still several years away from arriving at the front-line, the USAF meanwhile was about to receive its 'next-generation' air superiority fighter, that was to be NATO-assigned in Europe almost from the outset. When the 1st TFW at Langley AFB, Virginia took delivery of the McDonnell Douglas F-15A Eagle in January 1976, it received what was then the world's best air defence aircraft. The fighter's Pratt & Whitney F100 engines gave it an unequalled power-to-weight ratio and hence performance. It had a sophisticated new avionics suite, a potent array of weapons including Sparrow and Sidewinder air-to-air missiles, a Vulcan cannon and improved fire control systems.

By the end of 1976, the 1st TFW had been fully re-equipped with the Eagle, allowing the next batch of aircraft to be deployed to USAFE. In April 1977, the 36th TFW at Bitburg AB received its first F-15As, providing NATO with an air superiority fighter in the European theatre which could out-perform the latest Soviet MiG-25s. By October 1977 the Wing's third squadron had arrived at the base in Germany's forested Eifel region, after a working-up period at Langley AFB.

To help bring NATO air defence pilots up to a high peak of readiness, it was decided to form an 'aggressor' training unit. The 527th Tactical Fighter Training Aggressor Squadron (TFTAS) was formed at RAF Alconbury, with F-5E Tiger IIs. The squadron was tasked to provide dissimilar air combat instruction to give pilots first hand experience of the tactics likely to be employed by the Soviets in combat and how best to counter them. The unit started to work up in May 1976, and soon its 'customers' included aircraft from other European NATO nations, as well as USAFE units. Bitburg-based F-15s were regularly detached to Alconbury for aggressor training.

As a direct result of the increase in Soviet forces deployed throughout the Warsaw Pact states, it was decided to add more F-15s to USAFE's assets. These Eagles went to the 32nd TFS at Soesterberg AB in the Netherlands from September 1978. This unit had the unique position of being controlled by the Royal Netherlands Air Force and tasked specifically with Dutch air defence duties. A total of 98 F-15A/Bs were operating with both the 2nd and 4th ATAFs, at the heart of NATO's operational area, by the close of 1978.

Following the 36th TFW's retirement of its F-4s

Painted in psuedo-Soviet markings, this F-5E Tiger II was flown by the aggressor training squadron at RAF Alconbury, providing 'combat experience' for NATO fighter crews from mid-1976.

An A-10A Thunderbolt II close
support strike aircraft shows
its unusual configuration, with
high set twin turbofans aft of
the wing, slab wing and nose-
mounted rotary cannon.

in favour of the F-15, another wing also gave up its Phantoms in 1978. The 81st TFW at RAF Bentwaters received the first of a very different type of combat aircraft, the Fairchild Republic A-10A Thunderbolt II in July 1978. The 'Warthog' was the USAF's first specifically-designed close air support attack aircraft, with a formidable tank-killing capability thanks to its nose-mounted 30mm GAU-8 Avenger rotary cannon and AGM-65 Maverick missiles. Its deployment in support of NATO in Europe was the A-10's most important undertaking. The 'tank-buster' would have severely blunted or even halted any advance by Eastern Bloc tanks in the event of conflict developing.

The 81st TFW's A-10s were operational with six squadrons by the end of 1979, divided between the 'twin bases' of RAF Bentwaters and RAF Woodbridge, and strategically placed Forward Operating Locations (FOLs) in West Germany. The first of the four detachments was activated in May 1979 at Sembach AB, and rotational visits by a number of Thunderbolts to Ahlhorn, Leipheim and Nörvenich, as well as Sembach, became the normal operating pattern, placing the A-10 closer still to the potential battlefields of the Cold War. It also allowed more extensive exercises to be carried out in concert with the US Army's German-based Bell AH-1 HueyCobra attack helicopters. Equipped with TOW missiles, these battlefield helicopters were also operating in the anti-armour role.

By the end of 1979, USAFE's 81st TFW had six squadrons of A-10 'tank-busters' based at RAF Bentwaters and RAF Woodbridge.

The last USAFE wing operating Phantoms in the UK, the 48th TFW at RAF Lakenheath, started conversion to the General Dynamics F-111F from March 1977. This, the most powerful 'Aardvark' derivative to see service, equipped four squadrons at the base, receiving them from the 366th TFW at Mountain Home AFB, Idaho. The AN/AVQ-26 Pave Tack laser rangefinder and target designator pod was the variant's most significant feature, while Paveway laser-guided bombs provided the F-111F's primary weapon. Arrival of the 'F'. completed the F-111 strike force assigned to NATO in Europe, and with the type came the ability, if required, to attack targets with more precision than ever before.

A further new asset provided to NATO was the USAF's Boeing E-3A, which began operations with the 552nd Airborne Warning and Control Wing at Tinker AFB, Oklahoma in March 1977. Prior to this, the USAF had maintained a detachment of veteran Lockheed EC-121Ts from the 79th AW&CS, Air Force Reserve at NAS Keflavik, Iceland. The E-3's advanced airborne early warning facility became a key element in the development of NATO's superior integrated airborne warning and control system (AWACS). Having gained experience when NORAD personnel joined E-3 Tactical Air Command crews on missions in the USA, NATO had already decided to establish its own Alliance-wide AWACS/AEW

Right: US Army Bell AH-1S attack helicopters played a key part working with A-10s in the battlefield anti-armour role.

Below: F-111Fs replaced the USAF's last UK-based F-4s to enhance USAFE's precision strike capability. They were flown by four squadrons of the 48th TFW based at RAF Lakenheath from 1977.

capability. The RAF had a small number of piston-engined Shackleton AEW2s in the role, and was developing the ultimately ill-fated Nimrod AEW3 as a replacement. The NATO Defence Planning Committee first discussed the matter in the same month as the USAF E-3As entered service. Their proposal to form a NATO Airborne Early Warning Force equipped with 18 E-3A Sentries was finally approved in December 1978.

One of NATO's most important training programmes for its front-line pilots began in 1978, when Allied Forces Central Europe (AFCENT) established its Tactical Leadership Programme (TLP) at the Luftwaffe's Fürstenfeldbruck AB near Munich. The objective of the TLP was to develop closer inter-operability between the different NATO air arms. Initially comprising a two-week classroom-based course without any flying element, it was doubled in length in 1979 – staying in Germany, but moving to Jever and including a programme of actual simulated combat sorties involving aircraft from several NATO nations working together in a more practical application of inter-operability and sortie leadership. In the same year AFCENT began its biennial programme of Tactical Air Meets (TAMs). This combined the competitive Tactical Weapons Meet and *Royal Flush* exercises, but

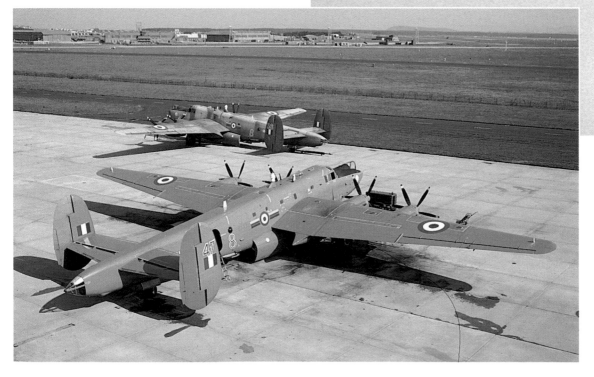

As a result of the Nimrod AEW3's failure to meet the required specification, No 8 Squadron, the RAF's airborne early warning unit, continued to operate these veteran piston-engined Shackleton AEW2s for this essential task.

abandoned the element of competition in favour of providing a more realistic environment for tactical training in Central Europe. At their home bases, NATO front-line units were also tested for their operational proficiency during TACEVALs (tactical evaluations), involving short-notice assessment by 'judges' from the Alliance. These would involve such elements as simulated airfield attacks on the units' home airfields, often by other air forces, and the response to each was closely assessed. In addition, further experience of working in conjunction with

other air arms within NATO was achieved by its programme of unit exchanges, which reached a particularly high and regular tempo during the late 1970s and early/mid-1980s. Apart from flying sorties, cross servicing by groundcrews at the host station of unfamiliar aircraft types began to make up a major element of these visits.

The French Air Force continued to participate in NATO exercises and exchanges in spite of not being a military member of the Alliance. By the end of the 1970s, three wings had received Mirage F1Cs

(ECTT30, EC5 and EC12) for the all-weather interceptor role, replacing the ageing Mirage IIIC, although the multi-role Mirage IIIE equipped elements of four units (EC2, EC3, EC4 and EC13) and the only Mirage VFs made up two squadrons of the latter wing. The Armée de l'Air's nuclear strike force was spearheaded by the Mirage IVA fleet, split between two wings, while its tactical attack capability, both nuclear and conventional, was provided by the Jaguar As of three units (part of EC3, plus EC7 and EC11). French involvement in the TLP, TAMs, TACEVALs and exchanges continued to be wide-ranging. In the case of the TLP, for instance, France was able to provide low-

level training airspace to NATO, while itself gaining the same amount of additional expertise during the course of these exercises.

Meanwhile, the question of how NATO should respond to the fast growing Soviet nuclear threat in the late 1970s was posing a real problem for analysts and planners. The extension of East-West détente which, it had been hoped, would develop through arms control talks, had faded in the light of the expansion of the USSR's forces, and the clear advances in missile technology, that was spreading across the Eastern bloc. Within NATO, a new Long-Term Defense Plan (LTDP), strongly advocated by US President Jimmy Carter, brought about increased

A picturesque German castle forms the backdrop for this low flying RF-4C, clearly identified as operating from Zweibrücken with USAFE's 26th Tactical Reconnaissance Wing.

Above right: French Air Force Mirage F1CRs continued to take part in exercises, along with other front-line types, despite France having withdrawn from NATO's military wing.

military spending and further force deployments.

The NATO Nuclear Planning Group met in April 1978 in Denmark, and noted that longer-range theatre nuclear weapons, in particular the SS-20 with its multiple warheads, were being deployed by the USSR in greater numbers. A series of important NATO meetings, by the Defence Planning Committee and the North Atlantic Council in 1978-79, laid down the foundations that were to enhance the Alliance's defensive posture in the longer term. A Special Meeting of Foreign and Defence Ministers in Brussels during December 1979, ratified proposals from the Defence Planning Committee for a 'modernisation' of the organisation's nuclear force in a new Flexible Response strategy.

As a result of this, the USA was to deploy Pershing II mobile intermediate-range ballistic and BGM-109 Gryphon cruise missiles to Europe – 108 of the former to be based in West Germany, while 464 of the latter were to be spread between locations in the UK, Italy, West Germany, the Netherlands and Belgium. At a time when doubts had been raised as to the strength of US defensive guarantees towards

Europe, the proposed deployment of American nuclear weapons was seen as confirmation of its commitment, as well as being cheaper than extending the alliance's conventional arsenal. Control of the nuclear missiles was left in US hands, to the dislike of some, but pressure from other NATO members had been brought successfully to bear on other issues relating to the missiles. In particular, the initial list of countries where cruise missiles were to be located was increased to include Italy, the Netherlands and Belgium, after representations from their respective governments.

A new complexion on these decisions was added only seven days after the end of NATO's discussions in Brussels, when on 21 December 1979, the Soviet Union invaded Afghanistan. Relations between the USSR and the West deteriorated still further, and a new period of heightened tension was generated. The fear amongst the West's political leaders was that too fierce a response to the situation in Afghanistan would end any hopes of future détente, and the all-important arms limitation measures. NATO was once again walking a tightrope.

TECHNOLOGY ADVANCES

Royal Norwegian Air Force General Dynamics F-16A Fighting Falcon

TECHNOLOGY ADVANCES

If the F-104 Starfighter symbolised NATO airpower in the 1960s, and the F-4 Phantom in the 1970s, it was the General Dynamics F-16 Fighting Falcon that carried this mantle through the 1980s. Initiated as a contender for the USAF's Lightweight Fighter (LWF) programme that required a maximum speed of Mach 1.6, an operational ceiling up to 40,000ft and a take-off weight under 20,000lb, the YF-16 was flown for the first time in 1974. Following a competitive fly-off against the Northrop YF-17, it was the F-16 that won through. With the LWF requirement changed to Air Combat Fighter (ACF), having the added provision for specific mission flexibility in foreign service, the new aircraft had a huge potential in the export market as a successor to the F-104.

On 7 June 1975, four European NATO nations (Belgium, Denmark, the Netherlands and Norway) jointly confirmed that they were to purchase the General Dynamics fighter alongside the USAF. The

Right: This Norwegian F-16A was built by Fokker at Amsterdam, one of 300 produced for this air arm and the Royal Netherlands Air Force.

A Belgian Air Force F-16A. Belgium was one of the four European NATO countries to initially order Fighting Falcons in 1975.

NATO air arms were all replacing their Starfighters with the new fighter, and in addition the Danes were also phasing out their last F-100s, the Dutch their NF-5s, and the Norwegians some of their F-5s, in favour of the F-16.

The initial F-16 order was for 348 aircraft – Belgium 116, Denmark 58, the Netherlands 102 and 72 for Norway. Of this total, 58 were to be two-seat F-16Bs. At the same time, it was announced that SABCA/SONACA at Gosselies in Belgium and Fokker in Amsterdam were to undertake licence production, assisted by around 30 suppliers in Europe. As with the earlier F-104 purchase by NATO members, the F-16 order was dubbed 'The Sale of the Century', although fewer countries were involved this time. West Germany was just receiving its F-4F Phantoms and had ordered the strike Tornado; Italy was also due to receive the latter aircraft, and had decided to keep its F-104s; Canada

had not yet decided on its CF-104 successor, and subsequently opted for the McDonnell Douglas F/A-18 Hornet. The RAF had also opted for the Tornado, keeping its Lightnings and Phantoms in service, and was still receiving Jaguars and Harriers.

It was not long before the European NATO orders were increased substantially. The Belgian Air Force increased its procurement to 136 F-16As and 24 F-16Bs, the Royal Danish Air Force to 54 and 16 respectively, the Royal Netherlands Air Force to 177 single-seaters and 36 two-seaters, and Norway raised its order to 96 'As and 14 'Bs. Apart from a handful built by General Dynamics itself, 221 F-16s rolled off SABCA/SONACA's line at Gosselies, most of which went to the Belgian and Danish air forces; and 300 were produced by Fokker in Amsterdam, the bulk of these for the Netherlands and Norway.

The capabilities of the F-16 were quickly enhanced. When General Dynamics' first full-scale development (FSD) aircraft flew in December 1976, it was able to carry 11,000lb of stores (3,000lb more than the original concept), while a computerised fly-by-wire system had been adopted to provide the type with still greater agility throughout the flight envelope. The F-16A's standard armament consisted of a 20mm M61A1 Vulcan cannon, with hardpoints able to carry such as AIM-9 Sidewinders, AGM-65 Mavericks and 500lb bombs, to a total of 15,200lb of ordnance.

The first unit to operate the F-16A/B, the USAF's 388th TFW at Hill AFB, received its initial batch of aircraft on 6 January 1979. Direct assignment of F-16s to NATO commenced only 23 days later, when the Belgian Air Force's first two-seat F-16B was delivered and Beauvechain-based 349 Smaldeel began its working-up process. On 6 June 1979, the

A second European F-16 line at Gosselies, Belgium produced this F-16B for the Royal Danish Air Force, one of 221 Fighting Falcons built there for Belgium and Denmark.

Royal Netherlands Air Force received its first two aircraft, with Nos 322 and 323 Squadrons at Leeuwarden changing from the air defence role to strike, to convert to the F-16. The following year Fighting Falcons went to the Royal Danish Air Force, serving initially with Esk 727 at Skyrdstrup, and the Royal Norwegian Air Force introduced them at Rygge with 332 Skv.

USAF F-16As were first seen in Europe during March 1981, when 12 aircraft from the 388th TFW deployed from Hill AFB to Norway in a demonstration of how NATO could be bolstered in Europe by 'reinforcements' from the continental USA. Six more F-16s participated in the Tactical Bombing Competition at RAF Lossiemouth that June, and easily surpassed the performance of all other participants in the attack element. The arrival

of the F-16 appreciably extended NATO's tactical strike and air defence capabilities. F-16As began to arrive with the USAF's 50th TFW at Hahn AB, West Germany in July 1982, replacing F-4Es, as they did with the Torrejon, Spain-based 401st TFW the following year. Alongside USAFE's F-16A/Bs, the Belgian Air Force had by this time two F-16 wings based at Beauvechain and Kleine Brogel; four Royal Danish Air Force squadrons now flew Fighting Falcons from Skyrdstrup and Aalborg; nine Royal Netherlands Air Force units either had or were soon to gain the F-16 at Leeuwarden, Volkel, Twenthe, Eindhoven and Gilze-Rijen; and four Royal Norwegian Air Force squadrons at Rygge, Bodø and Ørland were now combat-ready. The fighter now constituted NATO's most capable multi-role fighter-attack asset, both in terms of numerical strength and

Left: A Tornado GR1 in the colours of No 9 Squadron, the first RAF unit to become operational with the GR1 in mid-1982.

Above: The Marineflieger received West Germany's first Tornado IDS deliveries at Schleswig-Jagel, where MFG-2 was re-equipped by June 1982.

Right: With the introduction of the Tornado IDS, new weapons also appeared, like this MBB MW-1 airfield denial bomblet dispenser.

Left: A formation of British, German and Italian IDS Tornados from the unique Tri-National Tornado Training Establishment (TTTE) at RAF Cottesmore that was fully operational by April 1982, and continued to undertake pilot conversion training until March 1999.

its undoubted range of operational qualities.

Almost simultaneously with the F-16's development and introduction, the Panavia Tornado Interdictor/Strike (IDS) variant was progressing towards operational status. First flown in August 1974, 15 pre-production aircraft were used for a development programme by British Aerospace (formerly BAC), Messerschmitt Bolkow-Blohm and Aeritalia. This included rigorous testing of the navigation-attack system in conjunction with its fly-by-wire flight controls, especially in the low-level role which was to be the Tornado's forte. The first definitive production Tornado GR1 was flown at BAe's Warton facility in July 1979, at the start of an initial order for 640 IDS aircraft for Britain, Germany and Italy.

The first Tornado unit was the unique Tri-National Tornado Training Establishment (TTTE) that had been formed at RAF Cottesmore to undertake initial conversion training for all pilots onto the type. The TTTE's first aircraft – a pair of RAF GR1s – arrived in July 1980. West Germany started to build up its aircraft complement in September 1981, and Italy the following April. Weapons training remained the responsibility of the individual countries. The RAF's Tornado Weapons Conversion Unit/No 45 Squadron was established with GR1s at RAF Honington in June 1981; the Luftwaffe's Waffenausbildungskomponente formed at Erding five months later, and the AMI's weapons training was carried out by three squadrons, led by

154° Gruppo at Brescia-Ghedi, from February 1983.

The Tornado IDS was soon entering service with front-line units. No 9 Squadron at RAF Honington (previously a Vulcan squadron) received GR1s in January 1982 and became operational as the first RAF Tornado squadron in June. The Marineflieger put the first West German Tornados into service with MFG-2 at Schleswig-Jagel in mid-1982, but did not reach operational status with its MBB Kormoran anti-ship missile-equipped aircraft until the start of 1984. It was followed by the Luftwaffe's Nörvenich-based JBG-31 into full West German service, while in Italy 154° Gruppo was already up to strength.

With an increasing number of Tornado units being declared operational, NATO's strike force was rapidly gaining strength, and was further enhanced by the arrival of new weapons. Amongst the most important of these were to be the new airfield denial stores, led by the RAF's Hunting JP233 dispensers and West Germany's MBB MW-1 missile. Both of

these weapons would have been used against Warsaw Pact airfields in the event of air strikes commencing, and, in the case of the MW-1, for anti-armour sorties. In addition to the conventional weapons, the RAF's WE177 and the German and Italian B61 nuclear stores were also made available for use on the strike Tornado force. While the latter two air forces' IDS fleets were also armed with the AGM-65 Maverick missile, the RAF received Paveway laser-guided bombs for some of its GR1s. By the end of 1985, nine RAF squadrons were flying Tornado GR1s, six of them from Brüggen and Laarbrüch in Germany.

The Luftwaffe retired its last Fiat G-91R/3s from operational units as deliveries of the Dassault-Breguet/Dornier Alpha Jet A commenced in 1978-79. This Franco-German machine had initially been conceived as a replacement for the T-33 and Fouga Magister with training units, but a change in West German requirements led to it being adopted for the battlefield reconnaissance and light strike roles as well. Nearly 100 G-91s had remained in service with LeKG-41 at Husum and LeKG-43 at Oldenburg, as well as Fürstenfeldbruck-based WS-50, as weapons trainers. All of these units changed designations when the G-91s were replaced by Alpha Jets, becoming JBG-41, JBG-43 and JBG-49 respectively (the latter with training and ground attack elements), with no changes of base. Apart from the French Air Force's advanced and weapons training units flying Alpha Jet Es, the only other European operator of the type at this time was the Belgian Air Force. Some 33 examples were used by the Opleiding en Training Wing at Brustem-St Truiden.

NATO gained another new member nation on 30 May 1982, when Spain joined the Alliance following a formal application by the country's new government in December of the preceding year. This

Although conceived as an advanced trainer, the Dassault-Breguet/Dornier Alpha Jet was adopted by the Luftwaffe to replace the last of its Fiat G-91s in the light strike/battlefield reconnaissance roles.

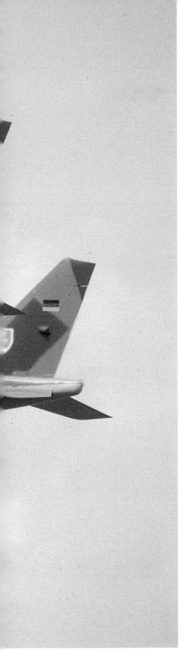

Formed at Geilenkirchen in 1982, NATO's multi-national Airborne Early Warning Force received the first of 18 Boeing E-3A Airborne Warning and Control System aircraft the same year.

took the number of member states to 16.

A very important development at this time was the establishment of the NATO Airborne Early Warning Force (NAEWF), formed at Geilenkirchen in Germany as a self-contained command, equipped with 18 Boeing E-3A Sentry Airborne Warning and Control System (AWACS) aircraft. The first E-3 was delivered in 1982, with the remainder following over the next three years. NATO decided to operate its AWACS fleet in Luxembourg markings, with the international crews being drawn from Belgium, Canada, Denmark, Greece, Italy, the Netherlands, Norway, Portugal, Turkey, the USA and Federal Germany.

During the early 1980s, the arrival in service of the Soviet Air Force's latest combat aircraft, and the continuing Russian presence in Afghanistan, was a cause for concern. In the Afghan theatre itself, the first deployment of the Su-25 *Frogfoot* demonstrated

that the Soviets now possessed a potent new battlefield close-support and tank-busting aircraft. Just as the A-10 would have supported NATO's armour, so the Su-25 was to fly alongside Warsaw Pact ground forces in their advance into the West. Based closest to NATO's borders were the two *Frogfoot* regiments in East Germany.

As NATO built up its capabilities in the high-speed, low-level tactical attack role, so the USSR's second generation of fighter aircraft were being replaced by a combat aircraft to match the West's F-15 and F-16. Frontal Aviation received its first MiG-29 *Fulcrums* during 1983, and soon a large number had been deployed with its regiments close to the frontiers of the Warsaw Pact countries. Not only was the *Fulcrum* an agile dogfighter, but the range of air-to-air weapons that it could carry and its combat radius made the new MiG a formidable opponent for NATO. One regiment each in Hungary

and Poland was re-equipped with MiG-29s, adding to the seven in East Germany and those 'at home' in the USSR.

In addition to the MiG-29 the Soviets began to undertake another major re-equipment programme, this time in its long-range interceptor force. In 1985-86, the PVO air defence command began to receive its first Sukhoi Su-27 *Flankers*. Later the new fighters were also assigned to Frontal Aviation, all of which were based in the USSR itself. With very long range, the Su-27 had the capability of escorting Soviet bombers right to the point of missile launch, against their designated targets. The *Flanker's* exceptional combat agility and provision for ten AA-10 *Alamo* and AA-11 *Archer* AAMs, or either unguided bombs or rockets, provided the Soviet Air Force with a powerful new offensive capacity. Ever

larger strike packages could now be launched, potentially including the latest production Tupolev Tu-95MS *Bear-Hs* of Long-Range Aviation carrying AS-15 (Rk-55) *Kent* cruise missiles.

Rather than having the agility to engage in close combat, the RAF's interceptor – the Panavia Tornado ADV – was intended to undertake 'beyond visual range' sorties against Soviet bombers in the defence of the northern and western flanks of NATO, and the UK Air Defence Region. Developed specifically for the RAF as a replacement for its Lightnings and Phantoms, the first prototype flew in October 1979, with interim Tornado F2s being delivered to the Operational Conversion Unit from November 1984. Unfortunately, problems associated with the Tornado's Foxhunter radar considerably delayed its introduction into operational service. As a result of

The Soviet MiG-29 *Fulcrum*, introduced into service with Frontal Aviation in 1983, and Warsaw Pact air forces in the following years, presented itself as a formidable adversary for NATO's F-15s and F-16s.

these delays and the Falklands experience in 1982, 15 surplus F-4J Phantoms were acquired from the US Navy to bolster the RAF's air defence capability. They were allotted to No 74 (Tiger) Squadron at RAF Wattisham and designated F-4J(UK)s – the only RAF Phantoms not powered by Rolls-Royce Spey engines.

Although the Tornado F3 entered service in July 1986, further delays, especially with the new radar, meant that the OCU had to be declared to SACEUR as being operationally-assigned before No 29 Squadron could 'officially' become combat-ready alongside it at RAF Coningsby. After 28 years front-line air defence service, the RAF's last Lightning F6s were finally retired in June 1988 by No 11 Squadron at Binbrook.

In the USA, the new McDonnell Douglas F/A-18 Hornet entered service with the US Marine Corps in August 1982, and the US Navy in March 1983. Early deployments were made to take part in NATO exercises, notably by VMFA-115 of the Marines who took F/A-18As to Denmark in 1986 for participation in Exercise *Northern Wedding*. Elements of the US Navy's Atlantic Fleet soon started to undertake cruises to the Mediterranean with Hornets aboard. The Hornet's APG-65 radar was far in advance of anything yet seen in either the air-to-air or air-to-ground roles, while its ability to carry AIM-9 Sidewinders and AIM-7 Sparrows alongside bombs of up to 2,000lb, plus AGM-88 HARM anti-radar, AGM-84 Harpoon ship-killing and AGM-65 Maverick missiles – with no performance penalties – was unequalled.

Qualities such as this attracted the Canadian Armed Forces to the Hornet, as a replacement for its CF-101 Voodoos, CF-104 Starfighters and CF-5

Below: One of the former US Navy Phantom F-4J(UK)s that equipped the RAF's No 74 Squadron at Wattisham after the Falklands War.

Left: Sunset for the RAF's
Lightning F6s. The entry into
service of the Tornado F3 in
1986 marked the beginning
of the end for the fighter
after nearly three decades
on the front line.

Above: Subject to delays,
mainly with its Foxhunter
radar and weapons system,
the Tornado F3 eventually
became fully operational on
NATO's strength in 1988.

Freedom Fighters. The initial aircraft of an order that was eventually to total 98 single-seat CF-188s (as the type was designated by the Canadians) were delivered to the conversion unit at CFB Cold Lake, Alberta in October 1982, while assignment to operational outfits began from early 1985 with No 425 Squadron at Bagotville, Quebec. This was the first of two NORAD-assigned air defence units to gain the CF-188, the other being located at Cold Lake, while both bases each hosted a NATO reinforcement unit which would have deployed to Lahr in Germany had an emergency situation developed in Europe. Hornet units permanently based with No 1 Canadian Air Division in Germany

were Nos 409, 421 and 439 Squadrons, all based at Baden-Söllingen.

Similarly, the Spanish Air Force, at this stage still only recently incorporated into NATO, was starting to receive its first EF-18A Hornets, which began to arrive with Grupo 15, at Zaragoza from July 1986 onwards. The new aircraft mainly replaced F-4C Phantoms (retired in 1979) and Mirage IIIs. The EF-18's dual-role capabilities allowed it to operate alongside the three squadrons of Mirage F1s already in service under Ala 14 and Ala 46 based at Albacete and Gando (Canary Islands). More recently, a number of surplus US Navy machines have been delivered to the EdA, allowing Grupo 21 at Moron

While the USAF opted for the F-16, the Canadian Armed Forces chose the McDonnell Douglas F/A-18 Hornet to replace its CF-5s, CF-101s and CF-104s.

These Hornets, designated CF-188s by the Canadians, were permanently based with No 1 Canadian Air Division at Baden-Söllingen in Germany.

to replace its ageing Northrop SF-5s with its two component squadrons.

Major changes in the US Army's aviation element in Europe occurred in 1987-88, with the arrival of the first McDonnell Douglas AH-64A Apaches in Germany. The initial assignments of this new, very potent attack helicopter, were to elements of the 1st Armored Division at Hanau and the 3rd Armored Division at Illesheim, where the AH-64 gradually replaced the AH-1S Cobra. Using advanced all-weather target acquisition/designation systems in conjunction with its AGM-114A Hellfire anti-tank missiles, the Apache soon demonstrated in NATO exercises its ability to work effectively as a 'team' with USAFE's A-10 Thunderbolt over the battlefield. US Army Europe remained NATO's largest helicopter operator, and its fleet of Sikorsky UH-60A Blackhawks also continued to grow, equipping medevac and assault units across West Germany.

At the same time, USAFE was adding the new

Left: A pair of F-4G *Wild Weasels* from the 52nd TFW at Spangdahlem in West Germany, the last USAF Phantoms to be permanently based in Europe.

F-16C Fighting Falcon to its inventory, starting in 1985 with the Ramstein-based 86th TFW and then, most significantly, equipping the 52nd TFW at Spangdahlem AB. With an improved F100 powerplant, advanced APG-68 radar and AGM-65D Maverick compatibility, this was effectively a 'second-generation' F-16. It also moved into the *Wild Weasel* role at Spangdahlem, operating alongside the Wing's F-4G Phantoms. The Fighting Falcon adopted the 'killer' role in the partnership, using its Vulcan cannon, bombs, cluster weapons and AGM-88 HARM missiles against enemy radar positions. The F-4Gs were now the last USAF Phantoms permanently based in Europe, after the 10th TRW disbanded at Alconbury and became the 10th TFW with two squadrons of A-10s. However, the recce Phantom was still occasionally seen in

Europe, as Air National Guard units undertook active-duty training (ACDUCTRA) and other deployments with NATO.

It was not all new equipment in NATO. With no replacement on the horizon, the Italian Air Force's long-serving F-104S Starfighters were put through an upgrade programme that would provide them with a new FIAR Setter radar, Selenia Aspide missile compatibility and a wide range of improved avionics. The AMI received 147 improved F-104S/ASAs by 1991 for service with seven squadrons.

The Federal German armed forces said farewell to the Starfighter in operational service during 1986-87 and the Navy ended F-104G operations with MFG-2 at Eggebek towards the end of 1986, when it received Tornado IDSs. The Luftwaffe's last front-line unit flying the type, Memmingen-based JBG-34, also switched to the Tornado. This did not mean that the F-104s were scrapped, as a number of them went into front-line service with the Turkish Air Force, the last of 137 ex-Luftwaffe F-104Gs and 33 TF-104Gs being delivered during 1988.

Another important new RAF Tornado variant, the reconnaissance GR1A, entered service with No 2 Squadron at RAF Laarbruch in 1988, marking the end of 13 years of continuous Jaguar operations in Germany as part of NATO's 2nd ATAF.

Meanwhile, the 'second-generation' Harrier GR5 began to be delivered to No 1 Squadron at RAF Wittering in November 1988. This Harrier II, developed with McDonnell Douglas, had major performance advantages over its GR3 predecessor thanks to its larger, carbon fibre wing, new lift-generating devices, and an uprated Rolls-Royce Pegasus engine. The interim GR5's greater and more diverse weapons load, that could be carried over a longer combat range and delivered with more accuracy, was a big step forward for the Harrier force. However, the RAF still had to wait for the full

night-attack version, the GR7, that was delayed while 'systems' were proved.

The new Harrier GR5 quickly followed into RAF Germany, equipping No 3 Squadron at Gütersloh from December 1988. With a longer range than the GR3, missions could now be undertaken much more effectively in support of British Army ground forces operating over a wider area. This 'battlefield interdiction' role gradually replaced the Harrier's original rather more limited 'close air support' role. Neither of the GR5 units were declared fully mission-capable to NATO until November 1989, when No 1 Squadron became fully-assigned.

With major political change occurring across Europe, the last years of the 1980s effectively ended the high pressure competition between NATO/USAF and the Warsaw Pact/Soviet Union, as the air arms attempted to match ever more costly technological advances on either side. In 1989 alone, the momentous events in Eastern Europe which had been threatening for some years started the process whereby NATO would no longer see the former Soviet Union and its Warsaw Pact allies as its principal adversaries. The die was being cast for major reductions in NATO's European-based strength and significant new tasks to be faced.

Above: An RAF Tornado GR1A in No 2 Squadron markings and temporary winter camouflage. This new reconnaissance variant replaced Jaguars at Laarbruch in 1988.

The much improved all-new
GR5 variant of the versatile
BAe Harrier first entered
service with No 1 Squadron
at RAF Wittering in 1988.

DRAMATIC CHANGES

Luftwaffe Mikoyan MiG-29 Fulcrum

DRAMATIC CHANGES

The events of 1989, NATO's 40th year, heralded the most dramatic period in European history since the end of World War 2, and were to alter the Alliance's shape and entire strategy over the next decade. The upheaval was the product of a series of social, political and military factors which together brought about change on an unprecedented scale.

Poland led the way as early as 1980, when unrest among workers led to the communist government under Prime Minister Jarulzelski permitting the establishment of trade unions. The Solidarity movement, headed by Lech Walesa, began to openly criticise the administration, leading to a series of labour strikes in 1981, and in spite of efforts at negotiation with the government, the situation worsened. Concern grew throughout the Warsaw Pact, and the USSR denounced the demonstrators for their attempts to break down communist rule.

With the threat of Soviet military intervention in Poland, as had previously happened in Hungary and Czechoslovakia, NATO made its own preparations. The USAF deployed four E-3 Sentries to Europe in

Below: Four USAF Boeing E-3Bs were deployed to Europe in 1981 to help monitor Warsaw Pact troop movements.

Huge batteries of these Soviet-provided surface-to-air missiles were located right across the communist East European states, as here near Bratislava.

early 1981 to monitor Warsaw Pact military movements; Exercise *Ocean Venture 81* was held in the North Atlantic during August and the annual *Reforger* exercise for ground forces with air support took on a new significance.

A rapid succession of Soviet leaders commenced in November 1982 with the death of Leonid Brezhnev. He was briefly replaced by Yuri Andropov and in turn, during February 1984, by Konstantin Chernenko, who was Soviet President for just 13 months. Waiting in the wings was Mikhail Gorbachev, named as Communist Party leader on 11 March 1985. A much younger man, he was known to have some inclination towards modernisation of the USSR as its economy began to slow down. Gorbachev was to preside over the most dramatic shift in Soviet policy and would oversee the events of 1989 which were to change the face of Europe.

The day after the arrival in power of the new Soviet leader, NATO began its latest round of arms control negotiations, that were to grow in scope and importance over the months to come. These began with the Geneva Disarmament Conference, followed later in 1985 by the recommencement of MBFR

discussions in Vienna, and, most significantly, the US-Soviet Nuclear and Space talks. Although there had never been so much negotiation before, there was relatively little belief in the West that any great change in the Soviet stance would come from them. Therefore the outcome of a meeting in September 1985 between President Reagan and the USSR's new Foreign Minister Eduard Shevardnadze came as a surprise, when, in the face of a US guarantee to adhere to the SALT II agreement of 1978 (unratified by the Americans) so long as the Soviets did likewise, Gorbachev rapidly proposed a 'cap' on Soviet SS-20 missile deployments and reductions of up to a half in the long-range missile forces of both the US and USSR.

Arms control talks continued over the following few months but without much real success. Accusations from both sides that the other had violated the SALT agreement; arguments over new weapons programmes and re-armament; and the continuing Soviet occupation of Afghanistan all saw to it that the conditions were not yet in place for a major sea change in the climate of superpower relations. However, Gorbachev was determined to improve East-West détente, and in 1986 put forward his own radical arms control proposals, while accepting the INF treaty's terms and agreeing to on-site verification inspections.

Gorbachev began to speak of *Perestroika*, a major programme of economic redevelopment, and *Glasnost*, a new Soviet political openness in both internal and external affairs. Significantly, the latter lent itself to furthering the arms control process through the adoption of a much more liberal attitude towards the West. This was viewed without the lingering suspicion which had remained in evidence during the new Soviet leader's first year in the Kremlin. The impasse over the proposed nuclear limitations measures continued to block progress until April 1986, with both the Americans and Soviets still dissatisfied with each other's proposals.

Gorbachev's primary drive was directed at removing the imbalance in conventional forces, not just within the NATO nations but taking in the whole area 'from the Atlantic to the Urals'. In October 1986, at a summit in Reykjavik, Iceland, a new agreement on START and INF was reached. Despite further stalemate on the Strategic Defense Initiative (SDI) – the US space-based Star Wars programme – another new proposal from Gorbachev to separate off the INF discussions speeded up progress, and this treaty was signed at the Washington summit in December 1987. This was a very significant step forward, since all long- and short-range intermediate nuclear weapons were to be destroyed (including the Soviet SS-20s).

In 1988, the Conventional Forces in Europe (CFE) discussions opened, during the early sessions of which the Soviets showed their willingness to concede that they would have to drastically cut back their ground forces in line with NATO's demands for equality. The Soviets were now starting to concede that their Cold War efforts at matching and exceeding NATO's force strengths had been overly belligerent. A new defensive thinking was coming to the fore as *Glasnost* and the reductions in military capability began to gain ground.

US President Ronald Reagan visited Moscow in May 1988 for an historic summit with Gorbachev during which he praised his counterpart's reforming zeal. A few years previously this would have been unthinkable – the leader of the major power in NATO engaged in friendly talks with the Soviet President, who was soon to withdraw his troops from Afghanistan, removing yet another barrier to progress.

As the USSR embraced the West as a new partner in negotiations and discarded hard-line communism, so it was seen as an opportunity for those in opposition to the governments of other Warsaw Pact nations to begin to do likewise. In Poland, demands for political change were growing by 1988-89. Mikhail Gorbachev's declaration that the USSR would not intervene with military action in the event of communist rule being threatened in any Eastern Bloc country, underlined the pace of change. Opening talks with the Solidarity movement sounded the death knell for Polish communism, as Walesa's organisation decisively won the first free elections in June 1989. Interim measures to keep Solidarity's leaders out of power failed, and one of its senior members, Tadeusz Mazowiccki, became Prime Minister in September with Lech Walesa as the new President.

In Hungary, a similar path was followed in 1988 as leadership of the Hungarian Communist Party and the post of Prime Minister were assumed by Károly Grosz who immediately set wide-reaching reforms in progress. A series of opposition parties formed which were, from their outset, clearly going to bring the end of communism in the nation. The Party renamed itself and disappeared from power.

The events were even more dramatic in East Germany during 1989. Through their access to West German TV and the slightly greater ability to travel to the neighbouring country, the DDR's citizens could see more readily how the other half of Germany lived. As they became increasingly frustrated at their state of affairs, events elsewhere began to clear the way for a change in the situation. Large-scale demonstrations began to take place in East Germany's major cities. The realisation that change was possible brought those who had long wished for the end of communism out onto the streets, along with a growing number of ordinary people who were now feeling that they had been enclosed in this system for too long. Leipzig was the first city to witness such a march, and soon afterwards a visit by Mikhail Gorbachev to East Berlin produced a warning from the Soviet President

Although the air forces of the Warsaw Pact were very well equipped with a wide range of capable aircraft, such as this East German MiG-21MF (top) and MiG-23ML (bottom), aircrews were not well trained in tactics and had restricted flying hours.

The USAF's SR-71A Blackbird reconnaissance aircraft was flown extensively from its European detachment base at RAF Mildenhall through the 1980s, monitoring the dramatic changes that were taking place. The advent of better military satellites and the abrupt end of the Cold War resulted in the SR-71's retirement in 1990.

to his East German counterpart Erich Honecker that he should not delay taking whatever steps towards reform were necessary. Without the possibility of help from the Soviets in maintaining communist power it was left to this increasingly-isolated administration to put down any disturbances on its own, and this nearly happened in Leipzig on 9 October. At the last minute, the decision was taken not to send the army into action, and when it became clear that no military opposition would be met on the streets of East Germany, the demonstrations grew in size and number.

More people left via Czechoslovakia, whose borders were soon opened to the West, and massive demonstrations in East Berlin and Leipzig put further pressure on the weakening government. On 9 November 1989, it was suddenly announced that all East Germans could travel abroad without restriction. The TV pictures from that night of the Berlin Wall being torn down were the most visible illustration of the end of the Cold War. The destruction of this long recognised symbol of the Iron Curtain and long years of conflict was flashed around the world. As preparations were made for free elections and the complete overhaul of East Germany's social and political systems, so it became clear that NATO would also have to adapt to this new political climate.

The final act in the incredible events of 1989 occurred during December, with the end of communism in Czechoslovakia. Although its leader, Milos Jakes, had remained steadfast against any

change, on seeing East Germany's government capitulate in the face of mounting public pressure, he attempted to move towards democracy. The new Civic Forum opposition group led mass protests and by December the communists had been ousted and dissident former playwright Václev Havel became president. Czechoslovakia's 'Velvet Revolution' removed the final bastion of Cold War politics from NATO's eastern frontier. Now, the discussions would start as to the future role of these nations alongside their Western neighbours.

Another major event occurred at midnight on 2/3 October 1990, when Germany was re-unified. Problems were to remain, but the DDR, for so long the Warsaw Pact nation closest to NATO's own central area of operations, had finally disappeared. As the USA and its Coalition allies prepared for conflict in the Persian Gulf, following Saddam Hussein's invasion of Kuwait in August 1990, NATO was faced with re-appraising its assets and strategies nearer to home in the post-Cold War era and the integration of a newly-united Germany into its structure.

The USAF was already looking ahead, and during 1990 two of its long-serving aircraft available to NATO were retired. In January, the Lockheed SR-71A was phased out of operational duties with the 9th Strategic Reconnaissance Wing at Beale AFB, California and its European operational detachment at RAF Mildenhall. Later in the year the *Looking Glass* continuous airborne alert posture, maintained for over 29 years by the 55th SRW's EC-135C

Right: Amongst the many aircraft that disappeared from Europe as the NATO air forces retrenched, was this Canadian Armed Forces Lockheed T-33A-N Silver Star that had been based in Germany for many years.

command posts, was ended, since the need for this active state of alert was no longer required.

Demonstrating the new priorities for the 1990s, the Bush administration's paper entitled 'Global Reach – Global Power', published in June 1990, outlined America's post-Cold War strategy. The new emphasis was to be placed upon force flexibility and 'smart' weapons technology, used to great effect before and during Operation *Desert Storm* which drove Iraqi forces from Kuwait in January-February 1991. The document's subsequent adoption led to major changes in the USAF's command structures from 1 June 1992, replacing MAC, SAC and TAC with two new organisations – Air Mobility Command and Air Combat Command.

The RAF quickly followed suit with a series of major organisational and equipment changes. Air defence of NATO's Second Tactical Air Force region, over Germany, was handed over to the Luftwaffe after 47 years. This brought about a surprising juxtaposition. Alongside the German Air Force's four wings of F-4F Phantoms that assumed the air defence task, there was now a squadron of MiG-29 *Fulcrums*. Based at Preschen and flying initially on

evaluation duties with JG-76, the former East German Air Force aircraft inherited from LSK/LV on re-unification became part of the front-line force as part of JG-73 in 1993. When first delivered to the DDR in May 1988, the 20 single-seat MiG-29As and four two-seat MiG-29UBs, were the first *Fulcrums* to serve with an air force outside the USSR. They moved to Laage in 1996 and have since been joined by JG-73's existing Phantoms.

When unification took place, the former East German forces' large inventory became part of the new united German armed forces. The old unit structures disappeared and many of its aircraft were grounded. Although most combat types were retired, examples of the Su-22, MiG-21, MiG-23 and Mi-24 were kept flying for evaluation purposes. Rather more of the transports and helicopters were pressed into Luftwaffe service, such as the An-26, Let 410, Tu-154 and Mi-8. The grounded aircraft were initially put into storage, but have since either been scrapped or sold to museums.

The RAF announced plans to cut back its forces in Germany initially by around half, with the Army making similar reductions. A single combined

The first of 20 single-seat MiG-29 *Fulcrums* inherited from East Germany after reunification, repainted in Luftwaffe colours and operated by JG-76, based at Laage.

An RAF Chipmunk making a farewell flight over the re-opened Brandenburg Gate in Berlin. A pair of the trainers was permanently based in the city to exercise the right to fly military aircraft over West Berlin in the days of the Cold War.

Above: The Luftwaffe took over responsibility for German air defence from 2 ATAF in 1990 using its F-4F Phantoms, augmented by the newly acquired MiG-29s.

Left: The Marineflieger also benefited from re-unification, operating a handful of Mil-8 helicopters for several years.

With Germany looking after its own air defence, the last RAF Phantom squadrons, Nos 19 and 92, were not required after 1991. Two aircraft were specially painted blue overall (right) in squadron markings to mark their departure.

squadron of support helicopters was to operate Pumas and Chinooks (No 18 Squadron); the number of Tornado GR1 squadrons was to be cut from seven to four at Brüggen and the two Phantom air defence squadrons withdrawn. No 92 Squadron left RAF Wildenrath in July 1991 and No 19 during January of the following year. The latter's final QRA 'scramble' occurred on 2 October 1991, just over a year after the Luftwaffe assumed responsibility for Germany's air defence.

Back in Britain, No 74 Squadron had relinquished its F-4J(UK)s, converting to surplus low-hours Phantom FGR2s in January 1991. It did not keep these long, as the famous 'Tiger' squadron, the RAF's last Phantom operator, was disbanded on 31 September 1992. It subsequently re-appeared as one of the Hawk training squadrons at No 4 FTS at RAF Valley. No 56 Squadron had earlier been disbanded as a Phantom fighter squadron and its number transferred to the Tornado F3 Operational Conversion Unit, but it retained its reserve NATO operational assignment. RAF Wattisham, having been home to these air defence squadrons, was closed and handed over to the Army Air Corps, as the new base for Nos 3 and 4 Regiments flying Lynx

and Gazelles, which in 1993-4 moved back to the UK from Soest and Detmold in Germany.

It was not all loss. The Boeing E-3D Sentry AEW1, the RAF's long-awaited replacement for its veteran Lossiemouth-based Shackletons, became operational at RAF Waddington with No 8 Squadron. At the same time, No 10 Squadron's fleet of cargo/passenger VC10 C1s were being given an additional flight refuelling capability to enhance the tanker force.

Another significant element in the NATO drawdown was the departure of the Canadian Armed Forces from Europe. No 1 CAD left Baden-Söllingen with its CF-188 Hornets and returned to Cold Lake, Alberta. Also leaving were the GTTF's veteran CT-133 Silver Stars from the same base, together with the CC-144 Challenger and CC-109 Cosmopolitan transport aircraft stationed at Lahr, and the co-located No 444 Squadron's CH-136 Kiowa helicopters. The Canadians completed their withdrawal from Germany in January 1993.

The new emphasis throughout NATO was henceforth to be focused upon rapid reaction to crises. It was clearly recognised in the Alliance's new

Strategic Concept that factors such as political instability, ethnic violence and economic breakdown would continue to pose real dangers, particularly during an extended period of change. While its main defence and augmentation/reinforcement forces were to have their states of readiness and inventories reduced, both immediate and rapid reaction forces took on a new importance, emphasising multi-national military flexibility in times of crisis.

Iraq's invasion of Kuwait in August 1990 prompted an enormous build-up of coalition aircraft at bases in the Middle East, acting under the auspices of the UN. Although not directly a NATO matter, the Organisation was called upon by Turkey to provide assistance in December 1990. Its government feared that Saddam Hussein's troops might attack its northern neighbour. As a result some 42 NATO combat aircraft were deployed by Allied Command Europe's Mobile Force (AMF) on 6-7 January 1991. These comprised 18 German Air Force Alpha Jet As, 18 Belgian Air Force Mirage Vs and six Italian Air Force RF-104G Starfighters. When it became clear that Operation *Desert Storm*

Above left: Following a cut in British Army personnel in Germany by nearly half, similar reductions were made by the RAF. No 18 Squadron received Pumas to operate alongside its Chinooks, as seen here. The squadron eventually returned to the UK.

Above: Army Air Corps
Lynx helicopters were also
withdrawn from Germany
as the troop reductions
were made. Nos 3 and 4
Regiments moved to
Wattisham, previously
an RAF Phantom base.

**Above: Army Air Corps
Lynx helicopters were also
withdrawn from Germany
as the troop reductions
were made. Nos 3 and 4
Regiments moved to
Wattisham, previously
an RAF Phantom base.**

was about to begin, further air defence equipment was sent to Turkey. With rapid control of Iraq's armed forces the AMF forces soon returned home, as UN combat aircraft took up residence as part of the peacekeeping effort.

In the Soviet Union, the declarations of independence by Estonia, Latvia and Lithuania in the spring of 1990 were met with opposition in Moscow, as Gorbachev attempted to hold the USSR together. They were followed later in the year by declarations of sovereignty by Armenia, Belarus,

Moldova, Tajikistan, the Ukraine and Uzbekistan, and then most significantly Russia itself, under the leader of its Supreme Soviet, Boris Yeltsin. As the Soviet economy became still weaker, conservative factions in the USSR's government joined with elements of the Army to launch a coup against Gorbachev, but resistance from Yeltsin and his supporters towards further reform won the day and the subsequent political arguments. Gorbachev had proposed the establishment of a Union of Sovereign States embracing all the former USSR republics

Above: A VC10 K3 of No 101 Squadron refuelling a pair of Tornado GR1s of No 617 Squadron. The services of the RAF's tanker fleet have been consistently in demand.

Left: After years of waiting, the first of the RAF's Boeing E-3D Sentry AEW1s entered service in mid-1991, finally replacing No 8 Squadron's elderly Shackleton AEW2s.

except the Baltic states, but Yeltsin met with the leaders of these nations and came to an agreement to create the Commonwealth of Independent States (CIS), with a much looser set of ties than had been the President's intention. Gorbachev's time in office ended on 8 December 1991.

This left the CFE agreement, which had been signed by the NATO and USSR leaders in November 1990, all but meaningless, since the forces that made up the totals were now split amongst the new republics. However, the agreement did set down all-encompassing new ceilings which would force the

CIS republics between them to cut back their total forces by some 50%, while NATO would only have to relinquish approximately 10% of its strength. Its prime aim remained – that of maintaining a balance of defensive capabilities on each 'side', while removing the offensive threat – but other factors were to determine the future strength of the once mighty Russian armed forces. NATO was soon looking to a major new crisis on its doorstep – not faced this time by the armed forces of a super-power with major political differences, but the much more insidious effects of ethnic tensions.

INTO ACTION

US Marine Corps McDonnell Douglas F/A-18D Hornet

INTO ACTION

The spectre of conflict in the Balkans has often hung over Europe. It reappeared once again in Yugoslavia in 1989, as a new mood of nationalism emerged in the republics of Slovenia, Croatia, Bosnia-Herzegovina and Macedonia. Serbian opposition to the break-up of the union was to be expected – Belgrade was the capital of both Serbia and Yugoslavia, and one-third of the Serbian people lived in the other republics. The Serbian president, Slobodan Milosevic, made it abundantly clear that unity would not easily be relinquished.

After WW2, the new multi-national state of Yugoslavia, created under Marshal Tito, comprised six republics (the old countries of Slovenia, Croatia, Bosnia-Herzegovina, Montenegro, Macedonia and Serbia) and two autonomous provinces (Vojvodina and Kosovo). This gave each nationality in the new state either a republic, or if the ethnic mix made this impossible to achieve, a province.

The events in Yugoslavia were not a direct by-product of the end of communism across Eastern Europe in 1989, since it had not been a member of the Soviet bloc for over 40 years. This was a new nationalism, with an overriding element of conflict based on historical fears. In the inter-war period, a Serbian royal dictatorship had effectively ruled over the region, persecuting Croats and Slovenes; fears grew that when the movement towards the break-up of Yugoslavia gained pace this would be repeated, bearing in mind the Serb wish for continued central control. On the other hand, during WW2 the Croatian NDH movement had taken brutal action against the Serbs, and now, as Croatia sought to gain independence, concerns mounted over the

Below: For three months in 1994, C-141B Starlifters of Air Mobility Command took part in the airbridge to the beleaguered city of Sarajevo, but when one aircraft received 22 bullets in its cockpit, the type was withdrawn in favour of the less vulnerable Hercules.

Above: Sarajevo in the rain. Humanitarian aid is unloaded from a USAF Hercules at the height of the war in October 1992.

possibility of violence being directed against the Serb minority in the Croatian Republic.

The people of Slovenia voted in favour of independence in September 1990, followed a year later by Croatia. The latter's referendum triggered intervention in both states by the Yugoslav Army, whereupon the international community, for many months preoccupied with matters in the Gulf, stepped in to push for an early resolution. It was the European Community that took the initial steps in this regard. By September, fighting in Slovenia was almost at an end, principally because there was no significant Serbian community there, unlike Croatia, where the conflict rapidly escalated. While the UN pursued negotiation towards a settlement, Serb forces besieged the city of Vukovar, and the Yugoslav Navy launched attacks on Dubrovnik and other parts of the Dalmatian coast. The UN's humanitarian agencies were by now becoming heavily involved in the plight of displaced people who had fled Croatia,

notably to Hungary. In February 1992, as fighting temporarily died down, the decision was taken to establish the UNPROFOR peacekeeping force of some 13,000 personnel.

However, conflict soon flared up in Bosnia-Herzegovina after it voted for independence in February 1992. Two months later, Bosnian Moslems and Croats were heavily engaged in fighting the Bosnian Serbs, and UNPROFOR observers sent to the city of Mostar had to withdraw. Soon there were over 500,000 refugees, with several major cities under siege by the Bosnian Serbs and Yugoslav troops. Among these was the capital, Sarajevo, where around 400,000 citizens required urgent relief. UNPROFOR's small presence there was constantly threatened by attack, and aid convoys sent by the UN High Commissioner for Refugees (UNHCR) were finding their task ever more dangerous. As attempts to halt the fighting were unsuccessful, efforts to deliver much-needed aid to Sarajevo and the rest of Bosnia were stepped up considerably.

Although operating under the control of the UN, several NATO air arms began aid flights into Sarajevo's airport after negotiations to re-open it were concluded in the summer of 1992. The huge airlift (named Operation *Provide Promise* by the USAF) commenced on 1 July and involved transport aircraft from 14 nations over the following three months. The flights involved a dangerous approach over territory being fiercely fought over by Bosnian and Serb forces, into an airfield 'watched over' by Mount Igman, another battle zone. It had to be executed as quickly and precisely as possible, with the minimum 'down time' for unloading, taxiing back out and departure. The French Air Force began the airlift with C-130Hs and Transall C-160s and was soon supported by USAFE C-130E Hercules from the 435th Airlift Wing and additional aircraft detached from the USA, operating from the 435th's

Below: The Italian Alenia G222 was one of the many transport aircraft used by the 14 nations involved in the huge airlift into Sarajevo. In September 1992, one of the type was shot down by a shoulder-fired SAM missile.

base at Rhein-Main, Germany. With primary 'hubs' at Split and Zagreb, German and Turkish Air Force Transalls, Italian Alenia G222s, Spanish CASA C-212 Aviocars, and Belgian, Canadian, Danish, Greek, Italian, Norwegian, RAF, Saudi Arabian, Spanish, Swedish and Turkish C-130 Hercules were soon heavily engaged in the airlift. In addition UNPROFOR chartered Russian and Ukrainian civil-operated Antonov An-12 *Cubs*.

Over 1,000 missions into the besieged Bosnian capital were completed by September, but the loss of an Italian G222 to a shoulder-fired SAM missile underlined the inherent dangers. The US Marine Corps combat search-and-rescue sortie deployed afterwards, using CH-53E Sea Stallions and AH-1W SuperCobras, was also attacked, though without loss. These events brought the *Provide Promise* effort to an abrupt halt in September. The airlift resumed the following month, with fewer participating nations, using aircraft fitted with self-defense equipment. The RAF, Canadian Forces, French Air Force, German Air Force and the USAF operated alongside the UN's chartered fleet and occasional involvement by other nations, including Sweden. The Joint Air Operations Cell at Ancona in Italy, moved from Zagreb, now administered the airlift, while UNPROFOR's nerve centre for Operation *Provide Promise* remained in the Croatian capital. In addition to the main airlift into Sarajevo, supplies were air-dropped into isolated regions of Bosnia from 28 February 1993. Initially using USAF C-130s operating from Rhein-Main, they were soon backed up by Luftwaffe Transall C-160Ds, flying from the same base. The airlift now proceeded without significant interruption.

Another feature of the conflict brought direct NATO involvement in October 1992. Yugoslav Air Force strikes on Croatian and Bosnian Moslem forces and communities using SOKO G-2A Galeb, G-4 Super Galeb, J-21 Jastreb and J-22 Orao attack

aircraft, and Mil Mi-8 helicopter gunships, was of increasing concern to the UN. As a result it was decided to establish a military no-fly zone (NFZ) over the country from 9 October 1992. The first aircraft deployed for Operation *Sky Monitor* were a pair of E-3A Sentries from the NATO AEW Force, subsequently joined by USAF E-3B/Cs, RAF Sentry AEW1s and newly-delivered French E-3Fs.

The decision to enforce the NFZ came after a series of violations during the latter months of 1992. As the E-3s monitored air and ground activity, plans were drawn up by NATO for greater involvement should the UN deem it necessary. Serb attacks on the town of Srebrenica in March 1993, including a

bombing raid by three veteran Antonov An-2s and numerous helicopter movements, brought the plan forward for action. The UN could not allow such flagrant abuse to continue, and at noon on 12 April Operation *Deny Flight* commenced, marking a new phase in the conflict.

NATO's combat air patrols (CAPs) involved aircraft from five nations, operating from bases in Italy. From USAFE, the 36th Fighter Wing at Bitburg deployed 12 F-15C Eagles to Aviano AB, while US Navy and Marine Corps F-14B Tomcats and F/A-18C Hornets joined from the USS *Theodore Roosevelt*. The USN also provided a squadron of A-6E Intruders for use in the close support role,

Most of USAFE's assets have been involved in operational flying over Yugoslavia, not least this 52nd FW F-16C (left) from Spangdahlem.

Below: US Navy Lockheed P-3C Orion maritime patrol aircraft based at Sigonella, Sicily, made many flights to monitor shipping in the Adriatic to ensure that UN embargoes were being maintained.

Right: French Air Force Mirage 2000s prepare for an Operation *Deny Flight* mission to enforce the UN No-Fly Zone in 1993.

along with E-2C Hawkeyes that gave AEW cover for the air drop flights. French Air Force Mirage 2000Cs from EC 005 at Orange took up residence at Cervia, and Twenthe-based No 315 Squadron, Royal Netherlands Air Force provided F-16A Fighting Falcons, operating out of Villafranca alongside six F-16A(R)s of No 306 Squadron at Volkel. Turkish Air Force F-16Cs, and RAF air defence Tornado F3s from No 11 Squadron flew out of Gioia del Colle. More Fighting Falcons arrived in July, as the F-15 Eagles returned to Bitburg in favour of 52nd FW Spangdahlem-based F-16Cs.

Controlling the NFZ enforcement operation was NATO's Fifth Allied Tactical Air Force, with its HQ at Vicenza. For 24 hours a day, seven days a week, two CAP areas, one around Mostar and Sarajevo, the other near Banja Luka and Tuzla, were patrolled. A typical four or five-hour sortie from Italy would require an hour's transit flying, an hour 'on station', a rendezvous with a tanker to refuel, before a further hour-long CAP, and return to base. The USAF's European Tanker Task Force provided air-to-air refuelling support for the USAF fighters, and other (Turkish and Dutch) F-16s engaged in *Deny Flight*.

Five KC-135R Stratotankers, at first provided by the 19th and 380th ARWs, were positioned on temporary duty at NAS Sigonella, Sicily. They were soon also able to replenish the US Navy's aircraft 'in theatre' by using probe-and-drogue attachments. The French Air Force sent a detachment of Boeing C-135FRs from ERV93 at Istres, one of which was involved in the first aircraft loss of the operation on its first night, when a drogue was ingested into a Mirage 2000C's engine intake. The RAF's tanker force from Brize Norton initially provided VC10 K2/K3s from No 101 Squadron, but these were soon replaced by No 216 Squadron Tristar K1s.

With the skies being constantly monitored by E-3s and the 24-hour CAPs, no combat aircraft from either side of the conflict were sighted in the NFZ for some months, although there were unauthorised helicopter movements, including three Bosnian Serb SA341 Gazelles on 14 May and a Croatian Mi-8 carrying ammunition the previous day.

NATO aircraft were also in action over the Adriatic in a separate operation enforcing the UN arms embargo on all of the former Yugoslav states, and the economic sanctions against Serbia and

Montenegro. Operation *Sharp Guard* involved US Navy P-3C Orions and Italian Air Force Br1150 Atlantics flying from Sigonella, along with French and German Navy Atlantic deployments to Cagliari in Sardinia. These were backed up by P-3s from the Spanish Air Force, Royal Netherlands Navy and Portuguese Air Force, as well as Canadian Forces CP-140 Auroras and RAF Nimrod MR2s. Armed patrols began in the summer of 1993 as Serbian submarines made what appeared to be threatening approaches to NATO naval vessels.

In the event of a ship suspected of carrying illegal arms being located, boarding parties could be landed on the offending vessel using naval helicopters. These included German Navy Lynx Mk 88s and Italian Navy Agusta-Bell AB212s, US Marine Corps CH-46E Sea Knights and CH-53E Sea Stallions, and UH-1Ns from the Marine Expeditionary Units. Royal Navy Sea King HC4s deployed with NATO and Sigonella-based US Navy CH-53Es of HC-4 were regular visitors to Allied ships in the Adriatic providing, logistic support.

In Macedonia, the number of UN monitors was increased in July 1993. The deployment of US Army Berlin Brigade troops to Skopje was carried out using USAF Hercules, StarLifters and Galaxies flying

In addition to US, Spanish, Portuguese and Dutch P-3s, the RAF provided Nimrod MR2s (above) and the Canadian Forces operated CP-140 Auroras (right) on patrols over the Adriatic and adjacent coastal areas during Operation *Sharp Guard*.

In-flight refuelling was provided for French Air Force fighters by C-135FR Stratotankers normally based at Istres.

out of Tegel Airport, Berlin. This was part of a major new effort to bring peace to the region, focused on Bosnia, where UN troops were stationed in the six 'safe havens' of Sarajevo, Srebrenica, Gorazde, Zepa, Bihac and Tuzla. These had been established in the wake of the spring Serbian offensive against Moslem strongholds, and the collapse of the peace plan put forward by Cyrus Vance and David Owen. Fighting escalated again, with Mostar coming under siege, attacks by Bosnian troops against Croatian enclaves, and a resumed series of Serb offensives on Mount Igman, overlooking Sarajevo. All of these met with no armed opposition from UNPROFOR, despite the fact that its mandate had been enhanced to permit the use of force if necessary in the event of attacks on its convoys or strikes against any of the UN-declared safe havens.

Air power was now available to protect UNPROFOR's humanitarian operations, a major new deterrent as part of *Deny Flight*. The first NATO strike aircraft, USAFE A-10A Thunderbolt IIs from the 52nd FW at Spangdahlem, arrived at Aviano, Italy during July 1993. The USS *America* was by now on station in the Adriatic, contributing A-6E Intruders and dual-role F/A-18C Hornets; US Marine Corps F/A-18Ds from VMFA(AW)533 made the first combat deployment of this all-weather night attack variant. A squadron of 12 Jaguar GR1As were sent to Gioia del Colle from RAF Coltishall, and both the French and Royal Netherlands Air Forces widened their *Deny Flight* commitments.

Further USAF deployments were subsequently made to support the operations. These were led by EC-130H Hercules from the 7th ACCS which moved into Aviano to provide command and control facilities. Brindisi had a sudden influx of Special Operations aircraft, beginning with four 16th SOS AC-130Hs that were used for night-time support of UN troops, as well as MH-53Js and HC-130s for various duties including combat search-and-rescue. The TDY detachment of KC-135s was doubled in

McDonnell Douglas F/A-18C Hornets aboard the USS *America* in the Adriatic are readied for action during Operation *Deliberate Force* in September 1995.

Above: Armed with overwing AIM-9L Sidewinder missiles, and carrying a variety of stores and a reconnaissance pod, this Jaguar GR1A of No 41 Squadron patrols over a snow-covered Bosnia.

Right: A US Navy Grumman E-2C Hawkeye 'mini-AWACS' returns to land on the USS *Theodore Roosevelt* after a mission over the no-fly zone.

size, and moved twice; firstly to Milan-Malpensa, then to Pisa.

During 1993, the presence of patrolling aircraft deterred the warring factions from impeding UNPROFOR. Their forces were able to directly call on air support, through Tactical Air Control Parties deployed with them, and this was regularly practised, as well as providing a visible deterrent. After a new Serb assault on Mount Igman and fierce battles near Mostar, and with the conflict clearly escalating, NATO strike aircraft took to the air above Sarajevo as a show of strength. On 27 August, a flight of A-10s followed suit over Mostar and US Navy A-6s prevented further shelling of the British Army base at Vitez with a similar 'display'.

While all this was happening, a number of changes were being made to the inventories of NATO air arms. In October 1993 the end of an era came when RAF Marham-based No 55 Squadron relinquished its last Victor K2 tankers, marking the end of operational service for the last of the 'V-bombers'. The RAF retired its last Buccaneer S2Bs in March 1994, with Nos 12 and 617 Squadrons at

Lossiemouth preparing for the arrival of Tornado GR1Bs for their maritime strike task. USAFE welcomed its first F-15E Strike Eagle deliveries for RAF Lakenheath's 48th FW from February 1992, equipping two of the previously four squadrons within the Wing. They replaced the last of the Wing's F-111Fs, which had previously been ferried back to the USA for storage. A year later the departure of the 20th FW's final F-111Es from RAF Upper Heyford spelt the end of the 'Aardvark's' USAFE service.

Spain's decision not to renew its Mutual Defense Assistance Agreement and insistence that the US cut back its presence there, led to the 401st FW moving its two squadrons of F-16Cs from Torrejon AB to Aviano, Italy, together with the co-located Headquarters of the 16th Air Force.

The Belgian Air Force's decision not to update 15 of its Mirage V fleet (comprising VBA attack and VBR recce versions) under the MIRSIP systems improvement programme led to the retirement of the type from 42 Smaldeel in December 1993. This left the air arm's front-line squadrons equipped

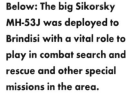

Below: The big Sikorsky MH-53J was deployed to Brindisi with a vital role to play in combat search and rescue and other special missions in the area.

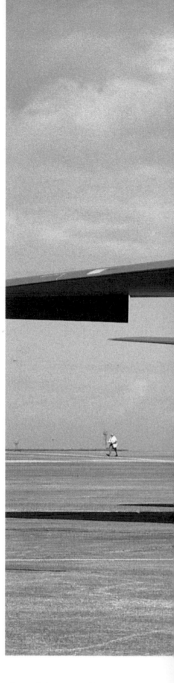

solely with F-16s. Like the Royal Netherlands Air Force, the BAF was affected by the post-Cold War cuts and domestic defence spending restrictions, and placed a number of Fighting Falcons in storage.

During the last two months of the preceding year, there had been a big changeover of USAF units involved in *Deny Flight*. Air Force Reserve and Air National Guard aircraft took the burden for a time, with a number of AFRes and ANG squadrons contributing crews to make up the A-10A deployment, while the Ramstein-based 86th Wing's F-16Cs (that replaced the 52nd FW's presence at Aviano in September) were relieved by Reservists.

A mortar was fired into a Sarajevo market on 5 February, causing 68 civilian casualties, whereupon the UN ordered the Bosnian Serbs to withdraw all heavy weapons within a 20km radius of the city.

Heavy air strikes were to be the penalty for non-compliance, and consequently NATO made further aircraft deployments to Italy. USAFE sent eight F-15E Strike Eagles to Aviano from RAF Lakenheath in the 48th FW's first operational deployment with the type. The French Air Force also substantially increased its Istrana-based commitment with Mirage F1CTs and Jaguar As, along with a contribution of Mirage F1CRs to the photo-reconnaissance force. Operating from the Adriatic, the French Navy carrier *Clemenceau* had Super Etendards embarked for strike and air defence duties, as well as reconnaissance Etendard IVPs. HMS *Ark Royal* was also on duty in the Adriatic with its RN Sea Harrier FRS1s from No 801 Squadron. When added to the attack and close support aircraft assets already assembled in Italy, this was now a formidable force.

Above: USAF F-15E Strike Eagles from the 48th FW at RAF Lakenheath were used on strike missions armed with Paveway laser guided bombs. During Operation *Deliberate Force* between August-September 1995, F-15Es spearheaded the bombing campaign.

On 28 February 1994, four Serbian G-4 Super Galebs, similar to this aircraft (right) were fired on by 86th FW F-16Cs over the no-fly zone – NATO's first ever air-to-air battle 'in anger'. Three of the G-4s were shot down and the fourth damaged.

Above: It is not surprising that the versatile A-10 Thunderbolt was deployed early on during Operation *Deny Flight*. This aircraft is moving in to take fuel from a USAF KC-135 tanker, on its return from a mission.

Deny Flight CAPs continued across the no-fly zone and it was one such patrol of 86th Wg F-16Cs that encountered a quartet of Serbian Super Galebs on 28 February. The 'intruders' were engaged in a bombing raid on Bosnian positions, and once detected by a NAEWF E-3A AWACS, had the Fighting Falcons vectored towards them to make an intercept. Following the bombing sortie by the Super Galebs, the NATO fighters were ordered to attack. The first was downed using an AIM-120A AMRAAM, the next two by AIM-9M Sidewinders, and the fourth was damaged by one of another pair of F-16s, again using a Sidewinder. This was the first

ever air-to-air combat engagement 'in anger' undertaken by NATO forces; it was also the first of the Bosnian conflict.

When Serb forces besieged the Moslem enclave of Gorazde early in April, NATO aircraft were soon in action again. Unarmed UN observers in the town were now under the protection of British SAS commandos, and they came under fire while on patrol. With calls for air strikes authorised much more promptly by the UN Secretary General's Special Representative in the theatre, Yasushi Akashi, he was quick to meet it with action. Via the command and control facilities provided by a USAF

Above right: Specialist aircraft like this *Commando Solo* EC-130E were brought in by the USAF to enhance airborne command and control facilities.

EC-130E and the forward air control capabilities of the UN ground forces, a pair of 86th Wing F-16Cs were directed to attack a Serb artillery command post. After this, normal patrols were resumed but the situation remained, so a day later two F/A-18s of the USMC carried out another strike.

This was effectively the last action for the 86th Wing, as its two F-16 squadrons soon moved permanently to Aviano, where they were re-numbered as part of the 31st FW. The transfer was complete in July, with the 510th FS and 555th FS soon being assigned to *Deny Flight*. After these changes, the 401st FW, which had moved from Torrejon to Aviano, gave up its F-16s and became the controlling unit for the USAF's detachments assigned to NATO operations at the Italian base. Renamed the 86th Airlift Wing, Ramstein's 'host unit' became USAFE's theatre transport provider, retaining its C-20A Gulfstreams and C-21A Learjets, but also taking on the 37th AS C-130Es from Rhein-Main, and the C-9A Nightingales used for aeromedical evacuation by the 75th AAS.

On 18 February 1994, the 52nd FW at Spangdahlem retired its last four *Wild Weasel* F-4G Phantom IIs that had been flown by the 81st FS. They were replaced by 18 F-15C/D Eagles for air defence. On 15 April, Bitburg AB, in Germany's Rheinland-Pfalz region, closed after 42 years at the heart of USAFE's commitment to NATO, and the 36th FW disbanded.

Back in the Balkans, problems around Gorazde worsened on 15 April 1994 when a French Navy Etendard IVP was hit by a Serbian SA-7 surface-to-air missile during a reconnaissance sortie, although it returned safely to the carrier *Clemenceau*. On the following day, NATO suffered its first aircraft loss 'in action' during *Deny Flight* when a Royal Navy Sea Harrier flying from HMS *Ark Royal* was shot down by a similar missile. The UN Commander in Bosnia, British Army Lt. Gen. Sir Michael Rose, instructed his forces in Gorazde to leave immediately, and a flight of French Army Light Aviation SA330B Pumas mounted a successful mission to extricate both the SAS troops and the Sea Harrier pilot, who had successfully ejected from his damaged aircraft. This was in preparation for possible air strikes on Serb forces around the town, but these were not necessary after a rapid Serb climbdown, after which an exclusion zone for heavy weapons was set up and 500 UN soldiers sent in to enforce it.

In the summer of 1994, Sarajevo's problems returned to the top of the agenda. Airlift operations into the city were halted for over three weeks, and Serb forces removed an anti-aircraft gun and two armoured vehicles from one of the UN's weapons control areas. In response, a strike was made on 5 August by two Massachusetts ANG A-10As from the 131st FS *Deny Flight* detachment, and on 22 September, after Serb gunfire damaged a French UN vehicle, a repeat attack was made by RAF Jaguars.

Despite these successful strikes against Serb armour the enforced closure of Sarajevo airport lasted into October.

Further fighting could not be prevented. In November, the Serbs launched a series of air strikes and a ground offensive on the Bihac enclave, and efforts to intercept the Galebs and Super Galebs being used were unsuccessful. However, NATO was soon permitted to attack the air base at Udbina from which the Serbian raids were launched. On 21 November the biggest NATO strike mission so far began with USMC F/A-18Ds of VMFA(AW)-332 knocking out the airfield's air defence systems using AGM-65 Maverick and AGM-88 HARM missiles. This was followed by ten F-16Cs from Aviano's 31st FW dropping CBU-87 cluster bombs to destroy taxiways, and 48th FW F-15Es pounding its runways with their GBU-12 laser-guided bombs. Further damage was done by French Air Force Mirage 2000Ns and RAF Jaguar GR1As.

The Udbina mission met its objective, but there was no easing of the overall Bosnian situation. Serbian SAMs now presented a greater danger, illustrated on 22 November when another RN Sea Harrier, on a reconnaissance sortie, had a 'very near miss'. To help give the patrolling aircraft greater protection, USAF EF-111A Ravens from the 429th ECS at Cannon AFB and USMC EA-6B Prowlers were deployed to provide radar jamming facilities, along with HARM-equipped F/A-18Ds to attack identified sites. On 23 November, the Serbs put a number of SAM radars into operation, which were promptly attacked successfully by NATO. Serbian forces then began a series of retaliatory measures against UNPROFOR, taking 300 soldiers hostage around Sarajevo, while besieging Bihac. F-15Es and F/A-18s took off from Aviano in another 30-strong strike package, but were called back after the guns fell silent.

This was to have been the end of NATO air

Below: Spanish Air Force EF-18 Hornets played an important part in all NATO air operations over Bosnia from December 1994, flying from Aviano AB in Italy.

Above: US Marine Corps EA-6B Prowlers, initially flying alongside the USAF's EF-111A Ravens providing electronic countermeasures over Bosnia, became the principal radar-jamming asset in the region, jointly operated by USAF, USN and USMC crews.

operations over Bosnia, as UNPROFOR felt that this constant presence was to an extent provoking the Serbs into further offensives. Humanitarian relief began to reach the country's people more easily once again, and the various factions declared a winter ceasefire. Unfortunately, this was by no means permanent, as Bosnian forces scored some successes against the Serbs, who responded with another seizure of weaponry from UN collection locations.

In April 1995, the UN airlift into Sarajevo ceased for six months, after gunfire hit a USAF C-130E on approach to land. When NATO's air presence over the city did not resolve matters, further strikes were ordered, this time against Pale (the Serb community's 'capital' in Bosnia). On 25 May, USAFE F-16Cs from the 31st FW, armed with LANTIRN night target acquisition pods and laser-guided weapons, and Spanish Air Force EF-18A Hornets, bombed

ammunition dumps. The Spanish Hornets from Ala 12 had first been deployed to Aviano the previous December, and were flying the first combat sorties by this air arm since the Spanish Civil War in 1936.

Another aircraft was lost to a Serbian SAM on 2 June, when an F-16C from the 31st FW was shot down near Banja Luka while engaged in a *Deny Flight* patrol. After successfully ejecting from his doomed aircraft, pilot Capt. Scott O'Grady managed to evade capture for nearly a week. His radio transmissions were picked up by NATO aircraft, and six days later the US Marine Corps launched a difficult rescue mission. Operating from USS *Kearsarge*, a CH-53E Super Stallion flew into the Bosnian Serb territory where O'Grady was hiding, and successfully extracted him. The big rescue helicopter was supported by AH-1W SuperCobras in the immediate vicinity, and AV-8B Harrier IIs

Lacking suitable aircraft, the RAF called for USAF assistance to transport 24 Airmobile Brigade's equipment and some of its personnel in Operation *Quick Lift* in July-August 1995. The Air Mobility Command C-5 Galaxies (top) and C-141 Starlifters (left) flew daily sorties from RAF Brize Norton.

Above: A fully armed US Marine Corps F/A-18D Hornet taking off from Aviano for a mission, with an RAF E-3D Sentry in the background.

provided close air support. They were joined in this role in the vicinity by F/A-18Ds of VMFA(AW)-533, and other patrolling NATO aircraft.

NATO's attacks near Pale met with a bloody response from the Serbs, who in one of the conflict's worst atrocities to date, shelled Tuzla and killed 75 civilians. When further air strikes hit more ammunition stores, 300 UN personnel were taken hostage and used as 'human shields', chained to strategically-important military targets. This did not last long, as NATO once more decided to suspend its attacks, but then in July the Moslem town of Srebrenica again found itself under Serbian fire. Strike aircraft patrols were launched to meet with any further advances, and on 11 July a pair of Royal Netherlands Air Force F-16As destroyed a tank and command post. With no UN troops left in the town, little more could be done to protect its inhabitants, and a large number of refugees desperately in need

of aid escaped to Tuzla. Another (non-NATO) air arm found itself involved at this point when the UNHCR made use of two Ukrainian Air Force Mil Mi-26 *Hook* heavy transport helicopters, as the best means of delivering supplies to the refugees.

Srebrenica's plight highlighted the need to bolster UN ground forces with a heavily-armed Rapid Reaction Force (RRF), the establishment of which had been initiated by France and Britain after the Pale hostage-taking. RAF Hercules transports made numerous flights to position a British Army artillery regiment 'in-theatre', but moves were delayed owing to various Croatian and Bosnian objections, the latter fearing that this was part of a UN withdrawal. USAF Air Mobility Command C-141B StarLifters and C-5 Galaxies transported 24 Airmobile Brigade and its 1,700 personnel from RAF Brize Norton during the month-long Operation *Quick Lift*, that ended in August 1995.

Above: The British Army Air Corps operated its helicopters, like this Lynx AH9 of 3 Regiment, from the new heliport at Ploce on the Croatian coast.

Left: As required by the UN, this RAF Chinook, in keeping with other UK and French support helicopters, was painted white overall to enable it to fly safely into Bosnian airspace.

An influx of helicopters arrived as part of the Anglo-French RRF. The British Army Air Corps provided 18 Gazelle AH1s and Lynx AH7/9s from 3 Regiment to augment the helicopters of No 664 Squadron AAC that had arrived in January. They were accompanied by six-strong detachments of RAF Puma HC1s from No 33 Squadron and Chinook HC2s of No 7 Squadron. A French Army contingent comprised seven SA330B Pumas and eight SA342M Gazelles, all operated by 5 RHCM. A new heliport at Ploce on the Croatian coast was used as the base for this rotary-wing fleet, though only those painted in the UN's overall white colour scheme were permitted to enter Bosnian airspace until the end of August. This also included the Royal Navy's four Sea King HC4s from No 845 NAS,

operating on UN duties from Split and Gornji Vakuf.

Two of the RAF Chinooks were sent to Pleso near Zagreb during August as part of a new humanitarian effort, caused by a Serb refugee exodus from the Krajina area after Croatian attacks. Ilyushin Il-76s chartered by the UNHCR flew aid into Belgrade, but the congestion caused by this mass of displaced people made road transport impossible, and the use of helicopters the only option. F/A-18Cs from the USS *Theodore Roosevelt* were used for a HARM attack on Serb radar at Krajina on 4 August, in what was to be the final strike mission in this phase of NATO's operations.

Anxious now to defend the UN's 'safe havens', after a Bosnian Serb mortar attack on a market in Sarajevo on 28 August killed 38 civilians, NATO

began Operation *Deliberate Force* in the early hours of 30 August 1995. This was by far the Alliance's biggest air offensive to date. USAF EC-130Hs and EF-111As were airborne first, jamming Serbian radar in support of the initial path-clearing strikes. These were launched from the USS *Theodore Roosevelt*, and comprised F/A-18C Hornets and EA-6B Prowlers, which knocked out the air defence network established around the Bosnian capital. This left the way open for the first waves of attacks on Serb offensive positions. Five strike packages executed precision raids during the opening phase, hitting various important military targets. Three more followed on 31 August, in an effort to force the Bosnian Serb military commander Gen. Ratko Mladic into withdrawing his heavy weapons in line with the UN's demands. However, after a break in air operations while a response was awaited, there was still no sign of movement on the Serbs' part.

The use of laser-guided weapons had meant that the majority of military targets around Sarajevo had been dealt with effectively and efficiently during the

Above left: Boom operator's view of a heavily armed F-15E Strike Eagle taking on fuel high over the Adriatic, en route to attack Serbian air defence installations.

US Navy F-14A Tomcats fitted with TARPS pods were primarily used for photo reconnaissance throughout the Bosnian conflict and subsequent NATO peacekeeping missions.

German (above) and Italian (left) IDS Tornados were deployed to take part in Operation *Deliberate Force* from September 1995. The Luftwaffe also supplied its 'new' Tornado ECRs, for the Suppression of Enemy Air Defences (SEAD) role.

opening two days of *Deliberate Force*. When it resumed on 5 September, a wider range of targets were to be hit, including Serbian command posts and bridges. During the next four days, a maximum of seven sorties per day were flown, all multi-national in their composition. The Aviano-based 31st FW F-16Cs spearheaded the effort, again using the all-weather laser target designation facility offered by their LANTIRN pods. Having participated in the first strikes around Sarajevo, armed with Paveway LGBs, the 48th FW's F-15Es now moved on to attack air defence installations using GBU-15 stand-off stores. Suppression of enemy air defences (SEAD) was undertaken by 429th ECS EF-111As, jamming hostile radars before they were put out of action in attacks by F-16Cs of the 52nd FW and their AGM-88 HARMs.

RAF Harrier GR7s had by this stage been deployed to Gioia del Colle by No 4 Squadron from Laarbrüch, Germany. This was the first operational use of the new night attack variant and they worked in conjunction with No 54 Squadron Jaguar GR1Bs that used the newly fitted TIALD pods to designate targets for the GR7s' Paveway laser guided bombs. Also participating were French Air Force Mirage 2000Ds fitted with AS30L laser-guided stores. A Mirage 2000N was the only NATO aircraft lost during *Deliberate Force*, when it was hit by a Serb SAM during the campaign's first night, its crew ejecting and being taken prisoner until December. No 322 Squadron of the Royal Netherlands Air Force and its F-16As made use of unguided iron bombs, and again the Spanish Air Force's EF-18As were heavily involved, operating with both HARMs and GBU-16 LGBs. Significantly, both the Italian and German Air Forces began their involvement at this time: the AMI's Tornado IDS force, provided by 6° Stormo and 36° Stormo, became involved in strike sorties; Luftwaffe Tornado ECRs of JBG-32 were engaged in SEAD and AKG-51's IDS Tornados

Right: A USAF 16th Special Operations Service (SOS) AC-130 Hercules 'gunship' takes on fuel from a KC-135 tanker of the 99th ARW based at Genoa, during Operation *Deliberate Force*.

The RAF has operated a photo-reconnaissance Canberra PR9 of No 39 (1 PRU) Squadron for medium/high-level missions over Bosnian territory almost continuously throughout the conflict, from Gioia del Colle.

in reconnaissance duties, in what was Germany's first combat deployment under NATO.

Deliberate Force also included A-10As from the 131st FS, Massachusetts ANG flying in support of UN ground forces. This mission was later augmented by attacks to 'clean up' remaining targets near Sarajevo, with over 180 sorties being flown in total. Similarly, the 16th SOS AC-130 'gunships' flew night air patrols over the city. Air-to-air refuelling was provided by KC-10A Extenders of the 9th ARS, equipped with both probe-and-drogue and boom systems for greater flexibility, and an increased number of 99th ARS KC-135s. Flying from Genoa, two tankers were always on station at any one time in a refuelling track over the Adriatic. Spanish KC-130s, RAF Tristars and a French C-135FR also took part in the air-to-air refuelling.

While the NATO, RAF and French E-3 Sentries monitored all *Deliberate Force* sorties, four EC-130Es deployed by the USAF's 42nd ACCS linked communications between the attacking fighter-bombers, forward air controllers and UN ground troops. The task of locating potential targets and providing details for post-strike damage assessment fell to a number of air arms. The Royal Netherlands Air Force used F-16A(R)s from No 306 Squadron, the US Navy provided F-14A Tomcats fitted with TARPS pods, flying from the USS *America*, and the French Air Force operated Mirage F1CRs. Higher level photo-reconnaissance over Bosnia was provided by an RAF Canberra PR9 of No 39 (1 PRU) Squadron based at Gioia del Colle, and the USAF's 9th RW Lockheed U-2S detachment carried out daily missions during the campaign flying from RAF Fairford. Also based in the UK, at RAF Mildenhall, RC-135s of the 55th Wing were among the aircraft that mounted electronic intelligence-gathering (ELINT) sorties alongside French Air Force DC-8 SARIGUEs, German Navy Atlantics from MFG-3 at Nordholz, and an RAF Nimrod R1 of No 51 Squadron, based at Pratica di Mare.

Deliberate Force's scope was further expanded on 9 September, when air defence installations near Banja Luka and other areas in north-west Bosnia were added to the list of targets. US Navy Tomahawk cruise missiles were used against some of these on the following day, the Serbs retaliating with attacks on UN troops around Tuzla. A request for air support was met by F/A-18C Hornets from VMFA-251 flying off USS *America*. Its Carrier Air Wing also included two US Navy squadrons of Hornets, VFA-82 and VFA-86, and they began to play their part in strike packages until the decision was taken to halt operations on 14 September. Gen. Mladic announced that the Serbs were to obey a negotiated ceasefire in Sarajevo, re-open land and air routes into the city, and withdraw the heavy weapons which had created the situation.

On 15 September 1995, the UN airlift into the Bosnian capital resumed after a gap of six months, with the arrival of a French Air Force C-130H from Ancona. Full operations recommenced the next day with flights by Canadian Forces, Luftwaffe, RAF and USAF transport aircraft. The steep 'Khe Sanh' tactical approach was adopted to keep arriving transport aircraft out of the line of fire from ground

Left: Lockheed U-2s of the
USAF's 9th Reconnaissance
Wing, initially based in the
UK at RAF Fairford and
subsequently moving to
Istres, France, flew daily
missions during Operation
Deliberate Force, and as
required through to the
present.

Above: As in all modern
campaigns, electronic
intelligence-gathering is
an important requirement,
and missions over Bosnia
were led by strangely
configured RC-135s from
the 55th Wing, flying from
RAF Mildenhall.

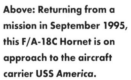

Above: Returning from a mission in September 1995, this F/A-18C Hornet is on approach to the aircraft carrier USS America.

A US Navy F/A-18C is readied for action aboard the USS *America* during Operation *Deliberate Force* in the autumn of 1995.

US Navy F/A-18C Hornets played a major part in the support of NATO operations over a long period. Ranged along the deck of the USS *America* (left) are Hornets of US Navy squadrons VFA-82 and VFA-86.

troops for as long as possible before touchdown. Meanwhile, NATO combat air patrols were used both to protect the airbridge and to continue to enforce the no-fly zone, especially during a renewed Bosnian and Croat campaign against Serbs in the west of the country. Serbian aircraft, operating from Banja Luka, started operating in defiance of the NFZ, but NATO aircraft, including 31st FW F-16Cs, RAF Tornado F3s of No 111 Squadron and Turkish AF F-16Cs soon forced them back onto the ground.

Other threats caused concern. UN forces became embroiled in a Serbian rocket attack on Bosnian troops near Tuzla on 8 October. A day later air strikes destroyed the position from which the

weapon had been fired, along with others nearby. This was to be the last sortie of its type, as some significant gains were made by the Croats and Bosnians throughout the country, reversing earlier Serb advances. The success of Operation *Deliberate Force* in removing the danger of Serb heavy weapons, grounding its air force and destroying their systems of military communications, cannot be underestimated as major factors towards the peace which began in November. After talks involving all the warring factions, the Dayton agreement signed in Paris on 14 December made provision for the UN's withdrawal from peacekeeping duties in favour of NATO's Implementation Force (IFOR).

KEEPING
THE PEACE

Royal Navy Westland Sea King HC4

KEEPING THE PEACE

More than 100,000 missions were flown by NATO aircraft in support of UNPROFOR during its involvement in the Bosnian conflict – 23,021 were *Deny Flight* combat air patrols; 27,077 close air support and strike missions (including 3,515 as part of *Deliberate Force*); 29,158 for operational support tasks such as air-to-air refuelling/airborne warning and control, and 21,164 were training assignments. NATO was given full responsibility for peacekeeping in Bosnia on 20 December 1995, when IFOR officially took over this responsibility from the United Nations on a year's mandate.

The UN wound down its operations over the closing months of 1995 and the beginning of 1996. This included the airlift into Sarajevo in which 21 countries had been involved, flying almost 13,000 sorties, to deliver some 160,000 metric tonnes of supplies, by the time of its official conclusion on 4 January. The airlift, which had been the longest-running humanitarian airbridge ever mounted, and the largest in terms of the amount of cargo delivered, actually continued until 9 January in order to empty the UN's food stores.

This was followed by a very different air transport effort by NATO – the deployment of IFOR troops, vehicles, helicopters and equipment into the theatre, replacing UNPROFOR's. Significantly, a number of East European nations were now working alongside NATO as part of the Alliance's Partnership for Peace (PfP) programme, providing major support by allowing IFOR the use of bases and sending their own troops to join the force. A total of 33 countries eventually participated, including 18 PfP participants from outside NATO. Amongst these was Russia, which became involved during January 1996.

An illustration of this came during the IFOR build-up phase. The US deployment, Operation *Joint Endeavor*, was initially focused on Rhein-Main AB in Germany. Marshalling areas around Rhein-

Main were filled with armoured vehicles, trucks, artillery and helicopters, as bad weather hampered plans to get them to Bosnia. It was decided to relocate the centre of US Army logistics operations to Taszar, a Hungarian Air Force front-line base for MiG-21s and Su-22s. From there, cargo was collected and taken by road via Croatia into north-west Bosnia, while vehicles and helicopters were flown to Tuzla, the main US base in Bosnia itself.

In addition to a large number of C-130E/H Hercules from the Ramstein-based 37th AS and US-based units and C-141B StarLifters, *Joint Endeavor* saw the major operational début of the USAF's latest transport – the C-17A Globemaster III. In December 1995, the 437th AW at Charleston AFB despatched the first complement of these big airlifters to Rhein-Main, 19 examples being used over the following three months. They flew hourly into Taszar and Tuzla on a daily basis, as part of a carefully-controlled, constant flow of movements in and out of both airfields. At Tuzla, where USAF transports arrived every half hour, danger remained. The hill overlooking the airfield still housed Serb artillery positions, and a large part of the base's own area was dotted with mines, making it unusable. Time was very much of the essence for the airlift operation, as only two aircraft could be on the restricted ramp space at once. At both bases, US Army helicopters were now present in some numbers – OH-58D Combat Scouts had been brought in by USAF transports from units in the USA, while those in Germany provided UH-60A Blackhawks and AH-64A Apaches.

Through 1996, over 60,000 troops were involved in IFOR's primary mission – to implement Annex 1A (military aspects) of the Peace Agreement. This involved separating the armed forces of the Bosnian-Croat Entity (the Federation) and the Bosnian Serb Entity (the Republika Srpska) by mid-January 1996; transferring areas between the two Entities by mid-March; and, finally, moving the Parties' forces and

In the first days of the IFOR mission, British artillery was moved to points along the old front lines where tension still existed, using Royal Navy Sea Kings and, as here, RAF Chinooks.

heavy weapons into approved sites, which was realised by the end of June. For the remainder of the year IFOR continued to patrol along the 1,400 km long demilitarised Inter-Entity Boundary Line and regularly inspected over 800 sites containing heavy weapons and other equipment. In carrying out these tasks it opened 2,500 km of roads, repaired or replaced over 60 bridges, and freed up Sarajevo airport and important railway lines. One important element was the support given to the Organisation for Security and Co-operation in Europe (OSCE) in preparing and conducting the elections held in Bosnia during September 1996.

IFOR's air component, under Operation *Decisive Endeavor*, comprised aircraft from 11 nations and the multi-national NAEWF, and a total of some

5,500 personnel provided by 13 countries. This was in addition to assets deployed to the region in direct support of the ground forces. Front-line fighter and strike aircraft remained on station and flew patrols over Bosnia, demonstrating to the former warring factions that NATO force was available to be used should any of them not have complied with implementation of the ceasefire agreement.

Once the September 1996 elections in Bosnia had been successfully completed, IFOR's UN-mandated task would be complete. However, with an unstable situation remaining in the area, NATO drew up plans for the continuation of its operations. It was decided that a two-year consolidation period was required and on the basis of this, NATO Foreign and Defence Ministers concluded that a reduced

Above: In December 1995, the USAF pressed its new C-17A Globemaster IIIs into service on the massive Operation *Joint Endeavor* deployment. For a period of three months the C-17s flew hourly into Taszar and Tuzla on a daily basis. Rapid turn-rounds and alert guarding were required, as the base at Tuzla was surrounded by Serb artillery.

Right: The airlift from Rhein-Main to Bosnia was the first operational test for the 19 C-17As of the 437th AW.

Left: With the difficulties experienced by ground transport, a large fleet of helicopters was much in demand. The British Army Air Corps made good use of its fast and versatile Westland Lynx AH7s; this trio are seen operating from Gornji Vakuf.

Below: The US Army had a large number of AH-64A Apaches assigned to IFOR, on constant readiness for action against offending armour.

Above: Even Marine Corps helicopters, like this Boeing Vertol CH-46E Sea Knight, were deployed ashore to support both IFOR and SFOR operations.

military presence could help to provide the stability that was necessary. This NATO Stabilisation Force (SFOR) was activated on 20 December 1996, the day on which the mandate given to IFOR expired.

SFOR's military tasks were to 'deter or prevent a resumption of hostilities or new threats to peace; consolidate IFOR's achievements, and promote a climate in which the peace process can continue to move forward'. In addition, it was also required to 'provide selective support to civilian organisations within its capabilities'. An 18-month period was initially envisaged for this, with NATO reviewing its force levels in relation to the overall situation a year before the intended conclusion in June 1998. The SFOR operation was named *Joint Guard*.

Overall military authority was placed in the hands of the Supreme Allied Commander Europe (SACEUR). About 35,000 troops were retained for SFOR's task in Bosnia, about half as many as had been allocated to IFOR. Every NATO nation with armed forces again committed troops, while Iceland, the only other member of the Organisation, provided medical support. In addition, the 14 Partnership for Peace nations – Albania, Austria, Bulgaria, Czech Republic, Estonia, Finland, Hungary, Latvia, Lithuania, Poland, Romania, Russia, Sweden and the Ukraine – continued their contribution to SFOR, along with Egypt, Jordan, Malaysia and Morocco. Slovenia and the Irish Republic brought the number of participating non-NATO nations to 20.

The OSCE began preparations for the Bosnian municipal elections in September 1997, for which SFOR was directed to provide a secure environment, as it was for the Sub-Regional Arms Control Agreement, limiting the holdings of heavy weapons in the region. The UNHCR's on-going effort to return refugees and displaced persons was given SFOR assistance by ensuring that none of the conflict's factions would return weapons into the Zone of Separation. Meanwhile, the support already provided by IFOR to the International Criminal Tribunal for the former Yugoslavia (ICTY) continued under SFOR. This included the provision of security and logistic support to ICTY investigative teams.

Operation *Deliberate Guard*, the air component of SFOR, had a smaller commitment than during the IFOR period, but still provided a powerful line-up of combat aircraft. By June 1998, when SFOR's original mandate concluded, around 31,800 sorties had been flown over Bosnia, mostly without incident. In addition, the force's helicopters had been heavily involved in assisting troops patrolling the 1,400 km-long Zone of Separation, monitoring 766 cantonment sites, compliance with de-mining and removal of unauthorised checkpoints. For all of these and other logistical tasks, NATO helicopters were used to assist with troop and equipment movements. Among the helicopters were RN Sea King HC4s and RAF Chinook HC2s based at Divulje Barracks in Croatia, alongside two Czech Air Force Mil Mi-17 *Hips*, the first aircraft from an East European air arm to become directly involved.

While peace was maintained in Bosnia, tension increased in Kosovo, one of the two autonomous provinces established just after WW2, where relations between the different ethnic groups had been deteriorating for some six years. In 1997, the long attempt by ethnic Albanians (nearly 90% of the population) to gain independence for Kosovo led to fighting against the much stronger Serb forces.

NATO aircrew, like those flying this RN Sea King HC4, had to fly in severe weather conditions to ensure that IFOR met the strict time-table for separating the warring factions, as laid down in the Dayton Peace Accords.

There were also numerous indiscriminate actions on the part of the Serbs and Yugoslav Army troops, described by the Serbian government as 'police actions' against the Albanian Kosovars.

NATO responded to the atrocities by a show of force in the skies over Macedonia and Albania involving combat and support aircraft from 11 nations. Exercise *Determined Falcon* on 15 June 1998 included 26 F-16A/Cs (from the Belgian, Danish, Dutch, Greek, Turkish and US Air Forces), ten Tornado IDS (Italian and German Air Forces), nine Jaguars (RAF and French Air Force), eight Spanish EF-18s, four US Marine Corps AV-8Bs, two Italian Tornado ADVs and two AMXs. Tanker support came from eight USAF KC-135Rs, two French C-135FRs, a Dutch KDC-10, a Spanish KC-130H and an RAF Tristar. A pair of NATO E-3As provided AEW support, while ELINT and electronic warfare tasks were met by a US Navy EP-3E Orion and two USMC EA-6B Prowlers. It was a very

impressive display, but the conflict continued.

When SFOR's original 18-month mandate concluded on 20 June 1998, it was clear that the armed conflict in Kosovo would need action by NATO to bring it to a halt. Over 300,000 people had been displaced from their homes in Kosovo and hundreds killed. The Alliance's SFOR 'follow-on' force was again slightly smaller than its predecessor but still a major commitment. No time limit was set for the end of Operation *Joint Forge*, as it was named. NATO's intention was to periodically assess the mission, with corresponding changes to the forces deployed according to the prevailing situation.

In an effort to intimidate ethnic Albanians in Pristina, the capital of Kosovo, a number of G-4 Super Galebs from the Yugoslav Republic Air Force began flying at low-level over the area during July, and 'buzzed' Kosovo Liberation Army (KLA) positions. Meanwhile, the US mediator, Richard Holbrooke, continued his efforts to promote a

Above: The Royal Navy's long stay in the Balkans continued with its Sea King helicopters playing a part in Operation *Joint Forge*, the continuation of the Alliance's SFOR commitment. They operated alongside RAF Chinook HC2s based at Divulje Barracks in Croatia.

Right: This Turkish Air Force F-16 was one of 26 Fighting Falcons that took part in Exercise *Determined Falcon* on 15 June 1998, when NATO put on a massive show of force over Albania and Macedonia.

ceasefire, but still no solution was forthcoming. NATO Secretary-General Javier Solana repeated his threat to use force to bring about an eventual political solution – especially with regard to Yugoslav leader Slobodan Milosevic's troops, and their offensives against the Albanians. Despite these warnings, fighting continued through July, August and into September. The last remaining ethnic separatist stronghold in Kosovo, to the west of Pristina, was attacked by Yugoslav and Serb forces on 22 September.

The Kosovo situation led to a new UN Security Council Resolution (1199) being adopted on 26 September 1998, demanding that all parties should end hostilities and maintain a ceasefire. In an attempt to enforce the resolution, the North Atlantic Council activated Operation *Determined Force*, allowing for 'limited air strikes' and a 'phased air campaign' in the event of non-compliance. NATO air arms rapidly began a large-scale mobilisation of forces – some 420 aircraft in all – led by the USAF, which sent six B-52H Stratofortresses of the 2nd BW

Spanish Air Force EF-18 Hornets (above) and Italian Air Force AMXs (left) were amongst the combat and support aircraft from 11 nations that participated in the aerial warning to the Serbs and Albanian Kosovars in June 1998.

Amongst the six nations that flew F-16s as part of Operation *Determined Force* was the Greek Air Force, with single-seat F-16As and this two-seat F-16B.

at Barksdale AFB to RAF Fairford on 11 October as part of a 250-strong commitment. These aircraft were to be armed with AGM-86C conventional cruise missiles. Two 509th BW B-2A Spirits were assigned for possible involvement, on standby at Whiteman AFB, Missouri, while a dozen F-117A Nighthawks from the 49th FW likewise remained 'on call' at Holloman AFB, New Mexico. These latter 'stealth' aircraft were to be based at Aviano, with its large number of hardened shelters, should their use have been required. This was the first occasion on which any of these three types had formed part of NATO's inventory for possible air operations in the Balkans.

Four Air Expeditionary Wings (Serbia) were formed by the USAF in support of its large-scale force from many different individual units which were based in Italy, Germany and the UK – the 16th AEW-SA (F-15Cs, B-52s, KC-135s and RC-135s); 31st AEW-SA (F-16Cs, A-10As, U-2s, KC-135s and EC-130s); 86th AEW-SA (KC-10s and C-130s); and the 100th AEW-SA (KC-135s). The F-15C Eagles were provided by the 493rd FS at RAF Lakenheath, but deployed to Cervia in order to leave Aviano's shelters clear for the possible arrival of F-117s that would operate alongside the 40 based F-16Cs of the 31st FW.

Other significant deployments included the French Navy aircraft carrier *Foch*, which was sent to

Left: The Royal Netherlands Air Force contributed to the tanker effort for the first time with the deployment of one of its pair of McDonnell Douglas KDC-10s from 334 Squadron at Eindhoven.

The deteriorating situation in Kosovo led to the USAF establishing four Air Expeditionary Wings (Serbia) to support its massive force, including the 100th AEW-SA under which this KC-135R from the 100th ARW at RAF Mildenhall was operated.

the Adriatic. It had 34 aircraft and helicopters embarked, including Etendard IVMPs (16F), Super Etendards (16F) and F-8P Crusaders (12F), with surveillance-gathering Br1050M Alizés (6F) and SA321G Super Frelon and SA365F Dauphin helicopters for transport and SAR duties. It joined the USS *Dwight D Eisenhower*, already on station as part of the US Navy's permanent carrier deployment to the region. Operation *Trident* was initiated by the French Air Force, which sent air defence Mirage 2000Cs, strike Mirage 2000Ds and Jaguar As to Istrana. Eight Royal Netherlands Air Force F-16As, newly-upgraded under the KLu's Mid-Life Update (MLU) programme, added to the eight already at Villafranca from Nos 322 and 323 Squadrons. The RAF provided four more Harrier GR7s from the Laarbruch squadrons (Nos 3 and 4), doubling the Gioia del Colle-based detachment. In all, 15 nations contributed to this build-up phase of *Determined Force*, officially activated on 13 October 1998.

The Yugoslav authorities were ordered to comply with the UN resolution within 96 hours of *Determined Force's* activation, while diplomatic negotiations between the US Special Ambassador, Richard Holbrooke and Yugoslav President Milosevic went on in Belgrade. They bore fruit two days later, when Milosevic agreed to a ceasefire and the withdrawal of his mobilised forces from Kosovo. An important outcome of this was to be the provision for an unarmed verification mission, with both ground and air elements (administered by the OSCE and NATO respectively) to check on compliance.

This produced yet another airborne programme – Operation *Eagle Eye*. Initially this comprised reconnaissance flights by USAF Lockheed U-2S aircraft from the 99th ERS, temporarily based at Aviano, from 16 October. These augmented and subsequently replaced the unmanned flights from Taszar, Hungary by the 11th ERS using the new RQ-1A Predator UAV. Operation *Eagle Eye* was soon expanded to include sorties flown by RAF Canberra PR9s flying out of Gioia del Colle, French Air Force Mirage IVPs from Mont de Marsan, French Navy Atlantique 2s and the US Navy's P-3C-III Orions, temporarily based at Sigonella.

After the negotiations had led to this initial agreement with President Milosevic, it was felt that further progress had to be made towards full

Left: Amongst the 420 NATO aircraft assigned to Operation *Determined Force* was this US Navy EP-3E for ELINT gathering, one of four permanently based with VQ-2 at NAF Sigonella, Italy.

Stratofortresses, like this B-52H, were deployed from Barksdale, Louisiana to RAF Fairford in October 1998 and again in February 1999, on standby for action in the Serbia-Kosovo stand-off.

compliance, and the 96-hour deadline imposed on the Yugoslav Republic should be extended to allow for further discussions, and give time for the departure of more forces. A new date of 27 October was set, by which Milosevic had to make progress towards peace and a drawdown of forces in Kosovo. As this latest deadline came closer, mounting evidence suggested that Serb forces were starting to heed the international community's demands, with troop withdrawals and no significant skirmishes between the warring factions.

NATO had seemingly achieved a settlement, but elected not to cut back its forces to any great degree, or alter the activation order for *Determined Force*. This turned out to be a wise decision. Some of the aircraft that had been deployed from the USA were stood down, most notably the 2nd BW B-52Hs which returned to their home base with their support aircraft (C-17s and additional KC-135s). The B-52 Stratofortresses at Barksdale were kept on alert, and were deployed again to RAF Fairford in February 1999.

Close monitoring of the situation on the ground was undertaken by the OSCE's Kosovo Diplomatic Observer Mission. These 2,000 unarmed observers were given a degree of protection, as the first of a projected 1,800 troops arrived in November. Forming an Intervention and Extraction Force (provided primarily by France) under Operation *Joint Guarantor*, they were based at Kumanovo in Macedonia. Although the observers reported that initially the agreement was holding, concern on the part of the UN, NATO and OSCE remained high. Both Serbs and Albanians carried out numerous violations of the October agreement, and in late November President Milosevic rejected the US proposal for Kosovo's future, on the grounds that this plan for 'broad self-rule' would have seen the Albanians gaining too much power over the minority Serb community. The KLA rebels' demands for full independence were unacceptable to all other parties.

Through December there were more breaches of the ceasefire. The worst incident occurred on 13 December, when 31 Albanians were killed during a battle with Yugoslav border guards, followed four days later by another major skirmish after a Serb attack on a rebel-controlled Kosovar village. Two

The backbone of the US
force were the 40 Aviano-
based F-16C Fighting
Falcons from the 31st FW,
temporarily re-assigned
as the 31st AEW-SA.

Left: A type new to the Balkans was the French Navy Breguet Alizé, normally based at Nimes-Garons, operating from the carrier *Foch*.

Above: French Navy F-8P Crusaders were amongst the complement of 34 aircraft and helicopters that were on board the *Foch* when it deployed to the Adriatic during the build-up of forces in the autumn 1998.

Left: This Lockheed U-2S from the 9th RW was deployed to Aviano (with the 9th ERS) on 16 October 1998, to make regular reconnaissance flights over the troubled area, under Operation *Eagle Eye*.

more ethnic strongholds, Podujevo and Obranca, then erupted into fierce fighting between 24-28 December before a fragile truce began, but as 1998 drew to a close it was becoming clear that any optimism expressed a couple of months previously now seemed ill-founded.

NATO's 50th anniversary year began with a decidedly ominous threat from the Serbian leadership, as it warned that they would use all means necessary against Kosovar rebels. The Alliance's presence in the theatre failed to deter the warring factions from launching into a new wave of violence: on 9 January 1999, Yugoslav and KLA troops clashed after eight of the former had been taken hostage by rebels, whereupon government forces started a push from Pristina towards the north.

The situation in Kosovo continued to deteriorate. The rebel killing of a Serb policeman near the village of Racak reportedly caused 15 KLA members to be shot in retaliation on 15 January; the same day saw the first attack on one of the OSCE's unarmed monitoring teams, by unidentified gunmen. Then, a day later, the bodies of 45 ethnic Albanians (some of them mutilated) were discovered in Racak, after the earlier Serb offensive. William Walker, head of the OSCE mission, was ordered by the government in Belgrade to leave Serbia, along with his 800-strong team, after he visited Racak and pinned the blame for the massacre on President Milosevic's security forces, but the monitors stood firm.

With support from Russia (traditionally an ally of Serbia) for the stance being taken by NATO, the

Left: The RAF added a
further four Harrier GR7s
to those already at Gioia
del Colle in 1999. Here
Laarbruch-based Harriers
take on fuel from a VC10
K3 of No 101 Squadron.

Under the title Operation
Trident, the French Air
Force increased its force,
including more Mirages
(right) at Istrana. The
French Navy contributed
a sophisticated Atlantique
2 (below) as part of the
reconnaissance effort for
Operation *Eagle Eye*.

North Atlantic Council decided on 20 January 1999 to increase the Alliance's military strength on standby for action, and further combat aircraft and ships were moved into the area. The USS *Enterprise* was relocated from the Mediterranean to the Adriatic, along with two escorting American warships, an additional destroyer, and other vessels attached to NATO's Standing Naval Force Mediterranean (STANAVFORMED). The French Navy carrier *Foch* returned to the Adriatic.

The readiness state for NATO aircraft in Italy was reduced to 48 hours from 96. Amongst the aircraft now available were four more RAF Harrier GR7s at Gioia del Colle; 12 USAFE F-15E Strike

Eagles from the 492nd FS, which replaced the Aviano-based 510th FS F-16Cs on *Determined Force* duties; more F-16s from Belgium, Denmark, the Netherlands and Norway; and a further 12 French Mirage 2000s. The Italian Air Force's provision was further extended with eight Tornado ADV/F3s from 36° and 53° Stormos being based together at Gioia del Colle, and a dozen F-104S/ASA Starfighters of 4°, 5° and 9° Stormos divided between Cervia, Amendola and Gioia respectively.

NATO troops and supporting units still in Bosnia and Croatia for Operation *Joint Forge* were also available for emergency use in Kosovo. These SFOR land forces were divided into three

Left: An RAF Chinook HC2 operating with 1310 Flight flying the mountainous route between its base at Split and the other major heliport at Gornji Vakuf.

multinational divisions: Multinational Division South West (MND/SW) with its headquarters at Banja Luka was led by the British Army and comprised elements from seven nations. Army Air Corps Gazelle AH1s and Lynx AH7/9s based at Gornji Vakuf operated in support, along with RAF Chinook HC2s and Royal Netherlands Air Force AH-64A Apaches, MBB BO105CBs and CH-47D Chinooks. These were also assigned to assist the

OSCE monitors, being based at Skopje in Macedonia. The Multinational Division South East (MND/SE) was under French Army leadership with contingents from seven other countries. Among the helicopters providing support were French Army SA330B Pumas and SA342M Gazelles, as well as German Army UH-1D Iroquois. Finally, the Multinational Division North (MND/N) came under the control of the US Army Task Force *Eagle*, based

One of a dozen additional F-104S/ASA Starfighters provided by the Italian Air Force, this one coming from 5° Stormo, normally based at Rimini.

at Tuzla. In February 1999, it had the largest number of helicopters to provide support, including AH-64A Apaches from US Army units based both in Germany and the USA, together with UH-60A Blackhawks, CH-47D Chinooks and OH-58D Combat Scouts.

With the situation at a stalemate, pressure was again mounted on both sides to resolve the conflict. French President Jacques Chirac met the British Prime Minister Tony Blair on 28 January, after which both leaders issued a statement denouncing the warring parties, and stated once more the fact that all options need to be considered. The following morning, British Foreign Secretary Robin Cook

(then Chairman of the Contact Group) stated that "we want to set a tight deadline for agreement...that would give free and fair elections for Kosovo, self-government, control over their own police and internal security... it would give Belgrade a way out of a conflict it cannot win". Both sides were given an ultimatum to meet for talks aimed at finding a way forward. These commenced in Paris at the beginning of February 1999 in the knowledge that a negotiated settlement, however difficult the process may be, had to be achieved. If this did not happen then it would appear likely that NATO air power would again be called upon in an attempt to bring peace to this part of the Balkans.

A NEW DAWN

Czech Air Force Mil Mi-24 *Hind*

A NEW DAWN

Whatever the outcome of the situation in Kosovo, there can be little doubt that NATO's attentions over the opening years of the new millennium will continue to be focused on the Balkans. There remain many different potential local flashpoints, and much 'unfinished business' is left to be done, not just by the Alliance but also by the OSCE and UN with NATO's assistance, in providing protection and logistics support.

While conflict continues in parts of the former Yugoslavia, co-operation between NATO and other East European nations, many of which were seen as potential enemies little more than a decade ago, has widened. Discussions began in earnest at the July 1990 London Summit, and by December 1991 the North Atlantic Co-Operation Council (NACC) had been formed. It met for the first time on 20 December, the 16 NATO members being joined by the Foreign Ministers of nine other nations. They laid down a strategy based on a new collectivity of affairs between the Alliance and these additional countries.

Its success clearly illustrated that an international body under NATO's auspices, which could forge much closer partnerships, was now not

Following the reunification of Germany in October 1990, the unusual situation of having Russian Air Force aircraft based in a NATO country was not finally resolved until nearly four years later. This Sukhoi Su-22M (below) is being prepared for its return flight to Russia.

Above: A Polish Air Force MiG-23 taxies out past a line of MiG-21s. In common with the air forces of its fellow former Warsaw Pact members, its equipment is largely of Russian origin, and it has taken over five years to bring its operation into line with NATO's air arms.

only desirable but also extremely realistic. In January 1994, the Alliance invited all the then NACC participant countries, and some additional OSCE member states, to join together to form a 'Partnership for Peace' (PfP).

In both political and military terms, PfP was intended from the outset to be a much more practical form of linkage between NATO and its new partners. The PfP facility was opened at NATO HQ in Brussels on 3 June 1994 and the Partnership's first joint training exercise, named *Co-operative Bridge*, was held near Poznan, Poland between 12-16 September, and involved soldiers from 13 NATO and PfP nations. Especially significant was the accession in June of Russia, following on from the start of a military co-operation programme involving exchanges and visits by senior commanders, as well as additional joint training.

Another important step was the final withdrawal of Allied troops from Berlin in September 1994, an occasion marked by the appropriate degree of

ceremony in the city. This followed the departure of the last Russian forces over the previous three years from the former Warsaw Pact countries – the 4th Air Army in Poland was disbanded at the close of 1992, and its remaining seven regiments – operating Su-24s, Su-27s, MiG-25RBs, Mi-24s, Mi-8s and various transports – had gone by August 1993. The Russian units based in the former East Germany (the unified country having, since 2-3 October 1990, been in the unique position of being a NATO country with Russian forces in situ) effected their withdrawal through 1993-94, with departures from numerous airfields: Falkenberg (MiG-29s), Welzow (Su-24MRs), Demin/Tutow (Su-25s) and Finow (MiG-29s) by June 1993; Templin (Su-17s and MiG-29s) and Damgarten (MiG-29s) in April 1994; Mahlwinkel (Mi-24s) and Oranienburg (Mi-6s and Mi-8s) during May-June 1994; and finally Sperenberg (Mi-24RKRs and Mi-8MTV/PS/TLs). The latter was the last German base with a resident Russian unit, and witnessed the disbandment on 27

May 1994 of the 16th Air Army which had controlled all Soviet/Russian operations in the DDR. President Boris Yeltsin flew to Berlin on 31 August, to mark the departure from Germany of the last Russian soldiers.

By the end of 1996, a total of 27 countries were members of PfP – Albania, Armenia, Austria, Azerbaijan, Belarus, Bulgaria, the Czech Republic, Estonia, Finland, Georgia, Hungary, Kazakhstan, Kyrgyzstan, Latvia, Lithuania, Macedonia, Moldova, Poland, Romania, Russia, Slovakia, Slovenia, Sweden, Switzerland, Turkmenistan, the Ukraine and Uzbekistan. Of these, 18 nations had already been involved in IFOR or SFOR operations in the former Yugoslavia. The next bold step would be to bring forward plans for the accession of three of the PfP nations to the status of full NATO members.

The 8-9 July 1997 meeting of the North Atlantic Council in Madrid issued a declaration confirming that the Czech Republic, Hungary and Poland had been invited to commence NATO accession talks, a decision described by the Alliance's Secretary-General, Javier Solana, as "a defining moment". He went on to say that "the Czech Republic, Hungary

and Poland have proven beyond a doubt that, as future allies, they will not only be consumers, but providers of security". After this expansion was announced, all three countries have brought their air defence systems, airfields and communications nearer to the standards required for membership, as well as continuing and furthering their PfP participation towards the desired level of inter-operability with other NATO forces.

All three nations were engaged in aircraft procurement programmes at the time of their accession. On 12 March 1999, the Czech Air Force announced an order for 72 Aero Vodochody L-159 light fighter/attack aircraft. Western types such as the F-16 and F/A-18 have been considered to replace the elderly MiG-21s, but have proved too costly. It is likely that the CzAF's Su-25K *Frogfoots* and Su-22M-4K *Fitters* will remain in service.

No decisions had been announced by March 1999 on the Hungarian Air Force fighter purchase, which had been deferred in 1996. The Polish Air Force also requires an updated fighter to replace its MiG-21s and to augment the its MiG-29A *Fulcrums* of which an additional ten aircraft were delivered to

Above: The Portuguese Air Force participated in the Partnership for Peace exercise Co-operative Key 98 with its F-16As, flying alongside Romanian MiG-21s, Slovak MiG-29s and Bulgarian Su-25Ks.

Right: Czech Air Force MiG-21s are likely to remain in service until a satisfactory purchase deal can be arranged for second-hand F-16s.

1 PLM in 1995 after the Czechs relinquished them. In return, the CzAF received 11 PZL-Swidnik W-3A Sokol transport helicopters, providing some welcome new equipment for the air arm's rotary-wing capability. The Polish Air Force is expected to lease or buy a small number of aircraft and is thought to favour the F-16 Fighting Falcon, with stored ex-USAF F-16A/Bs likely to meet this interim requirement. Consideration is being given to the ultimate purchase of F-16Cs, although the SAAB JAS39 Gripen and F/A-18 Hornet have also been closely assessed.

A problem shared by the Czech, Hungarian and Polish air arms and common across the other East European nations, is their aircrews' lack of flying hours and essential experience. This is a matter of some concern to NATO, whose stated aim is for pilots to have at least 128 hours flying time every year. In Poland for example, the figure is estimated to be just above 60 hours at present. This made the participation of the three new Alliance members in PfP exercises all the more valuable as a means of increasing inter-operability with other nations. The Partnership's exercise programme has been substantially widened to accommodate this.

The PfP organised its biggest air exercise, named *Co-operative Key 98*, in July 1998. Organised by AFSOUTH and located at three different locations in central Turkey, a total of 43 aircraft from six NATO and eight other countries were involved. With the emphasis placed on aspects of peacekeeping operations, it took in medical evacuation, airdrop, close air support and air defence tasks, including the simulated enforcement of no-fly zones. The list of participating aircraft illustrates its diversity: F-16Cs of USAFE's 555th FS, Bulgarian Air Force Su-25Ks, French Mirage 2000Cs, Italian F-104S/ASAs, Portuguese F-16As, Romanian MiG-21MFs, Slovak MiG-29As and Turkish F-16Cs made up the front-line force, while Bulgaria, Italy, Moldova, Romania, Slovakia and Turkey contributed transport aircraft and helicopters.

After the success of *CK98*, the opportunity was taken to build on the air transport aspects of PfP

The E-3A Sentries of NATO's
AEW Force have recently been
upgraded. This modified E-3
now has ESM sensors in side-
mounted canoe-type fairings
and chin mounted FLIR.

co-operation at RAF St Mawgan during Exercise *Co-operative Bear 98* in September 1998. Two RAF Hercules C1s, a Czech An-26, Dutch Fokker 60, French CN235, Latvian L-410UVP, Lithuanian An-26, Norwegian C-130H, Polish An-26, Romanian C-130B, Slovak An-26 and Swedish C-130/Tp84 took part, with teams from each country being involved in sorties representing the delivery of humanitarian aid and casualty evacuation. These two exercises formed the basis for further and extended activities by the PfP members over the coming years.

Direct co-operation between NATO member nations has continued under the auspices of the NAEWF and its operations have been refined through its major commitment to the Alliance's air forces engaged in the long-running Balkan conflict. Twelve nations fund the AEW Force (Belgium, Canada, Denmark, Germany, Greece, Italy, Luxembourg, the Netherlands, Norway, Portugal, Turkey and the USA), all of whom – except Luxembourg, whose registrations the aircraft carry – contribute crews to operate the 17 E-3A Sentries which remain based at Geilenkirchen, Germany. The NAEWF now has three Forward Operating Bases – at Preveza in Greece (where the fleet suffered its only aircraft loss, in 1996), Trapani in Italy and Konya in Turkey, along with a Forward Operating Location at Ørland, Norway. Its E-3As are divided between three operational component squadrons, as well as a fourth for training duties. The latter has three Boeing 707-329Cs used for conversion and support transport purposes and is to receive four additional ex-Luftwaffe 707s in 1999/2000. The RAF's two E-3D squadrons, Nos 8 and 23 based at Waddington, are also committed directly to NATO. The NAEWF remains the largest commonly-funded acquisition programme undertaken by the Alliance and is the only NATO-owned, multinational, operational force which is fully integrated into the command structure.

At the July 1997 Madrid Summit, France announced that it was not going to renew its membership of the military structures of the Alliance once more for the first time since de Gaulle's withdrawal in 1966. It has, for the moment at least, decided that the benefits of re-joining are not great enough to justify the outlay, mainly

referring to the budget set aside each year by every member which goes towards the Alliance's common funds. France continues to participate in the Organisation's joint exercises and plays a significant part in its operations in the former Yugoslavia.

The Czechs, Hungarians and Poles look set to be followed into the Alliance by a number of other countries from Eastern Europe. Secretary-General Javier Solana affirmed that "enlargement is not a one-off process. NATO's door will remain open to other aspirants who are willing to take on the responsibilities and obligations of membership...". His comment that the accession process will be reviewed at the Organisation's 50th Anniversary Summit in Washington, DC during April 1999 suggests that further expansion is imminent. Romania, Slovenia and possibly Slovakia are viewed as the most likely countries to be invited to join, probably followed by Estonia, Latvia and Lithuania that have had their prospective candidatures approved already, though no formal steps have yet been taken.

Moves towards military modernisation and closer integration with NATO have already been made by all of these nations. The Romanian Air Force, for example, is receiving upgraded MiG-21MF Lancers (being modified domestically by Aerostar and Elbit) and has modernised its transport fleet with the delivery of ex-USAF C-130B Hercules. 15 Brigada of the Slovenian Air Force, currently its sole operating unit, is receiving more new-build Pilatus PC-9s. The Slovak Air Force's plans are less certain, but it is known to have a requirement for further MiG-29s, possibly from surplus machines held by Mikoyan, and is upgrading its Mil Mi-24s. While no major re-equipment programmes are planned by any of the three Baltic states, they are having increased active involvement in the PfP.

Most of the NATO nations are carefully looking to the future and have announced plans to

These RN Sea Harrier FA2s of 801 Naval Air Squadron, photographed in February 1999 flying from their base at Yeovilton, will be moving to RAF Wittering/Cottesmore by 2003, as part of 'Joint Force 2000'.

rationalise, and in most cases reduce, their armed forces, in the light of the constraints and new challenges of the post-Cold War world. The British government's Strategic Defence Review (SDR), announced by Secretary of State for Defence George Robertson in July 1998 placed a great deal of emphasis on Joint Rapid Reaction Forces. The Army Air Corps' new WAH-64D Apaches will be part of a new Air Cavalry Brigade, while the support helicopter units of the AAC, RAF and Royal Navy are to be combined into a Joint Helicopter Command in which the RAF's new Merlin HC3s will form an important part. Continuing this theme, RN Sea Harrier FA2s and RAF Harrier GR7s will make up the 'Joint Force 2000', with much closer integration of operations building upon the degree of inter-operability already achieved.

The RAF's new links with the French Air Force through the Franco-British European Air Group highlights the efforts being made in several cases to create ties between different air arms. This is all the more significant as multi-national operations assume an ever-greater part of NATO's role. Such links are also being created as a result of defence cutbacks, notably in the case of the Belgian and Royal Netherlands Air Forces which have both seen the premature storage and (so far unsuccessful) offer for sale of a number of their F-16A/Bs. Plans have recently been announced which see the two air forces' F-16s alternately sharing weekend air defence QRA duties. The Benelux Deployable Air Task Force, established in September 1996, involves F-16s, FAB/BLu C-130Hs, KLu C-130H-30s, KDC-10s and Fokker 60UTA-Ns, Dutch Hawk and Patriot missiles, and Luxembourg Army troops, forming a quickly-deployable package in support of the UN, Western European Union, OSCE or NATO.

Training is another area in which several of the Alliance's air arms have already joined, or are to combine, their assets. The Euro-NATO programme

has been operated by the USAF for some years using T-38A Talons to instruct Dutch and German pilots, but now the NATO Flying Training in Canada (NFTC) organisation is being set up at the Canadian Forces bases at Moose Jaw and Cold Lake. Operated by Bombardier Services, 24 Raytheon T-6A (CT-156) Harvard IIs and 18 BAe Hawk 115s have been ordered for the basic and advanced elements of the syllabus for pilots of the Canadian Forces. It was announced in September 1998 that the Royal Danish Air Force is to be the first overseas customer for the NFTC.

Looking ahead to the new front-line aircraft types due to enter service with NATO air arms during the first decade of the new millennium, there are a number of long-running international procurement programmes of great importance. The Eurofighter Typhoon is probably the most significant of these, with four nations' air forces awaiting the type as their next-generation combat aircraft, with the possibility of other orders within the Alliance following. The RAF plans to obtain 232 Typhoons to replace the Tornado F3, and subsequently its Jaguars; the Luftwaffe requires 180, with 140 to replace F-4Fs and the remaining 40 its older IDS Tornados; the Italian Air Force is purchasing 121, as an F-104 and Tornado ADV/F3 successor, and the Spanish Air Force some 87, to allow retirement of its Mirage F1s. The first deliveries of the Eurofighter Typhoon are expected to commence in 2002-3.

Strong competition in other fighter 'markets' within NATO is guaranteed. The Saab JAS39 Gripen is being promoted strongly by BAe and the Swedish manufacturer amongst East European nations. Its relative simplicity and low cost make it an attractive and better-value long-term alternative to such as the F-16, F/A-18 or the much more costly next-generation types such as the Typhoon. Also potentially in the frame with some of these NATO customers is the Dassault Rafale, now well-

The Eurofighter Typhoon, here refuelling from a VC10 K3 of No 101 Squadron during trials, should enter RAF service in 2003, initially to replace Tornado F3s.

Left: Having been subject to an extended development period, the Dassault Rafale, first flown in 1986, has yet to enter service with the French Air Force or Navy. The Rafale M is expected to replace French Navy F-8P Crusaders in 2001.

FREEDOM OF THE SKIES : A NEW DAWN

Above: Already in service with the Swedish Air Force, the Saab Gripen is being vigorously marketed to NATO air arms in a joint operation by BAe and Saab, the main focus being on East European air arms.

advanced in its flight test programme and set to enter Aéronavale service in 2001, with deliveries following to the Armée de l'Air in 2003-4.

The USAF is focusing its re-equipment plans on the Lockheed Martin/Boeing F-22A Raptor. This advanced next-generation fighter, which combines the latest stealth technology with a new integrated weapons system, will carry new AIM-120C AMRAAMs and AIM-9X AAMs. Currently, the US Air Force expects to receive 339 Raptors, with the first unit expected to take delivery of the type (as an F-15 replacement) in 2004.

There are three major pan-European helicopter programmes that are set to add significantly to NATO's capabilities – at the battlefield front-line, in support of ground forces and at sea. While the Army

Air Corps has selected the GKN Westland-built WAH-64D Apache to meet its attack helicopter needs, both the French and German armies will take delivery of the Eurocopter Tiger in two variants, one for anti-tank and one for escort and support duties. The RAF's support helicopter force will be significantly enhanced by the introduction of EH Industries Merlin HC3 to No 28 Squadron at RAF Benson in 2000. Already being delivered to the Royal Navy at Culdrose, the Merlin HM1 is a well-equipped anti-submarine version. Italian Navy deliveries will comprise ASW, AEW and transport EH101 variants. The fourth new helicopter being supplied to NATO air arms – the NH Industries NH90 utility helicopter – is to be supplied to France, Germany and Italy, with navalised examples for the Netherlands.

Future transport aircraft requirements are also being assessed by many of the NATO air arms. The RAF is taking delivery of the first of 25 new C-130J Hercules late in 1999. The Italian and US Air Forces have also ordered C-130Js, and it is likely that other current operators of the C-130 will order the new version in due course. Submissions for the RAF's second tranche of transport acquisitions include the C-130J, C-17A, Antonov An-124 and the Airbus Future Large Aircraft (FLA), renamed the Airbus A400M in February 1999. This turboprop aircraft has been designed to meet the stated requirement of eight European air forces for their next generation of strategic and tactical military airlifters.

Plans reported a few years ago for a joint NATO pool of E-8 J-STARS, in the manner of the NAEWF's E-3A operations, have now been rejected, but an alternative currently appears to be a possibility. This would be along the same lines as the UK Ministry of Defence's ASTOR battlefield surveillance aircraft programme, expected to have been finalised during the summer of 1999. Lockheed Martin and Northrop Grumman are basing their bids around the Gulfstream V, with Raytheon using the Bombardier Global Express as its platform. Once the RAF order is made, it has been reported that NATO could form its own joint force using whichever aircraft is selected.

Looking further into the future, the US Joint Strike Fighter (JSF) will undoubtedly play an important part in NATO's line-up in the second decade of the new millennium. The Lockheed Martin X-35 and Boeing's X-32 will be evaluated for this programme in a competitive fly-off. The winner will become the key element of US tactical aircraft modernisation plans, with 2,852 set to be procured for the USAF, Navy and Marine Corps. There are to be three separate variants - a conventional take-off and landing (CTOL) aircraft for the USAF, a carrier-capable version for the USN, and the advanced short take-off and vertical landing (ASTOVL) derivative developed for the USMC but in which both the Navy and Air Force have now expressed interest. The latter is likely to be purchased by the Royal Navy, for operation as part of the RAF/RN Joint Force operating from the new Royal Navy carriers that are expected to be built.

Where does NATO see a potential future enemy coming from? A clue as to the Alliance's thoughts on this matter comes from its plans for a new strategic doctrine, being discussed by foreign ministers early in 1999. It refers to providing 'security in and for the entire transatlantic area', supported by the new partnerships being established with former Soviet republics which will provide NATO with influence as far as central Asia. The importance of a properly-co-ordinated rapid reaction capability to attacks by weapons of mass destruction will be recognised by the establishment of a dedicated section at the Organisation's HQ. Whether it is a terrorist group or a national government, more potential dangers at different levels have appeared during the last decade of the 20th century. There have already been gas attacks on subways in major cities and the threat of nuclear attack by rogue groups or from unstable countries has increased substantially.

There remain other concerns as well for NATO, not entirely unconnected with this. While the East-West conflict of the Cold War years may have ended, the lack of stability in Russia and some other parts of the former USSR remains a source of concern. If the continued efforts at financial and political reform in Russia fail, then the likelihood of disenchantment among the country's people and a potential rise of hard-line nationalism and/or communism will be all the greater. This could effectively turn the clock back 20 or more years, with all the consequences for the West that such an outcome would inevitably bring. It is hoped that,

Right (top): The USAF's next generation of fighters will include the Lockheed Martin/Boeing F-22A Raptor, the first of which is expected to enter service in 2004, as an F-15 Eagle replacement.

Right (bottom): The US Joint Strike Fighter project is being planned as a replacement for a wide range of tactical aircraft, including the F-16, Harrier, Sea Harrier, F/A-18 Hornet and Tornado IDS. The Boeing X-32 and Lockheed Martin's X-35 are contenders for a potentially huge order.

Below: Integration of flight systems and avionics has been the principal cause of the two-year delay in getting the first of 25 new Lockheed Martin C-130J Hercules into service with the RAF at Lyneham.

with the West's help, the economic crisis in Russia will be lessened, and thereby the chances of major political change diminished.

The fact that NATO's new strategic doctrine neither defines nor limits the Organisation's boundaries of operation is significant. It affirms the view that uncertainty and potential conflict could occur anywhere, and that forces must be available to react swiftly to areas of threat. In addition, plans for stronger European involvement in the Alliance when compared with that of the US have been welcomed. NATO has had to adapt to the climate of the post-Cold War world, with new areas of concern outside the boundaries of the old East-West conflict which existed throughout the Alliance's first 40 years. It has recognised that, while threats in its 'traditional' area of operations remain, the twin forces of unpredictability and instability are the real problems that it must cope with. As its 50th anniversary is reached, the North Atlantic Treaty Organisation seems set to play an ever greater role in the 'new world order' in the opening decade of the 21st century.

NATO TIGERS

Royal Air Force BAe Hawk T1

NATO TIGERS

Close links between NATO's air arms over the Alliance's 50 years have been promoted through many means. Programmes of regular deployments, unit exchanges and exercises have helped to develop multi-national inter-operability. The value of this was graphically illustrated during operations over the former Yugoslavia, when the experience gained was rapidly translated into combat action. One distinctive and quite unique part of the international relationship that has grown up across and beyond the Alliance, bringing aircraft and pilots together, has been the NATO Tiger Association.

The roots of this colourful association go back to 1960. The French Minister of Defence, Pierre Messner, wanted to enhance military co-operation between his country and the US, and as a result the Commander-in-Chief of US European Command (USEUCOM) suggested to all units under his control that they should attempt to build inter-squadron links. At the same time, the RAF's No 74 Squadron, that flew Lightning F1s from Coltishall, was rebuilding old wartime ties with USAFE's 79th Tactical Fighter Squadron based at RAF Woodbridge with F-100D Super Sabres. Both of these UK-based squadrons had a 'big cat' in their unit badges. When news of Messner's plea reached them, the 79th TFS undertook to find a unit of the French *Armée de l'Air* that had a theme that was shared with the two UK-based squadrons. They found that Escadron de Chasse 1/12 from Cambrai-Epinoy, equipped with the Dassault Mystère IVA, also had a tiger as its emblem, and the unit was promptly invited to join No 74 Squadron and the 79th TFS at Woodbridge during July 1961, for what was to be the first ever Tiger Meet.

The following year, the 79th TFS was among eight 'Tiger Squadrons' from six nations that gathered at RAF Upper Heyford. The established annual Meet moved out of the UK for the first time in 1963 when it was arranged by 31 Smaldeel of the

No 74 'Tiger' Squadron Lightning F1As at Coltishall. In July 1961, No 74 joined with the 79th TFS at Woodbridge and the French Air Force's Escadron de Chasse 1/12 at Cambrai, to hold the first Tiger Meet, at RAF Woodbridge.

Belgian Air Force at Kleine Brogel. A week-long programme of tactical flying exercises, combined with tasks for groundcrews, including cross servicing of a variety of aircraft types, culminated in a big social gathering and open day, as the established pattern of events. At the 1977 Tiger Meet held at RAF Greenham Common during the International Air Tattoo, the *Silver Tiger Trophy* was donated to the Association by London silversmiths Mappin & Webb. This fine award has been presented at each subsequent gathering to the tiger squadron showing the highest professionalism and greatest spirit at that year's meet. In spite of the 1970s fuel crisis, which forced the cancellation of the flying elements, the Association continued to flourish. The airborne element recommenced at Baden-Söllingen in 1983.

As the Cold War ended, so NATO and the individual air arms involved began to question the merits of the Tiger Association. In addition, three long-standing member units disbanded – No 439 Squadron of the Canadian Forces, 1/JBG-43 from the German Air Force, and the USAF's 79th FS (although only temporarily in the case of the latter). However, little could dampen the 'tiger' spirit, and major operational exercises are still arranged at most years' meets. In addition, the Tiger Association has itself adapted to the new climate in which the

It was fortunate that one of the Canadian Armed Forces F-104 squadrons based in Europe – 439 Squadron at Baden Söllingen – was eligible to join the Tiger Association. Its yellow and black tiger-striped aircraft attracted a good deal of attention, as here at the International Air Tattoo at RAF Greenham Common in 1977.

No 313 Squadron, Royal Netherlands Air Force, a new member in 1990, had the tail of this F-16B painted with a magnificent tiger's head, to mark its attendance at subsequent Tiger meets.

Left: The 1991 Tiger Meet, held at RAF Fairford during the International Air Tattoo, brought together a wide range of specially painted aircraft, including (top) an Italian Air Force F-104S/ASA from 21° Gruppo (a member since 1968), with a French Air Force Mirage F1 of EC1/12 (a founder member) behind. Also from France, this pink-nosed and overall tiger-striped Fouga Magister (left) was particularly colourful.

Before the Czechoslovak Air Force split, 11 SLP based at Zatec became an honorary member of the Tiger Association. One of the unit's MiG-29s is seen at the 1991 meet at Fairford, with a tiger striped fin.

Alliance operates, demonstrated graphically in 1991 when No 74 Squadron RAF F-4J(UK) Phantoms arrived at the Tiger Meet, hosted at RAF Fairford by the International Air Tattoo, in formation with Czechoslovak Air Force MiG-29As and L-39 Albatroses from 11 SLP at Zatec, another unit with a 'tiger' emblem. It's successor in the Czech Air Force, 41.slt at Caslav, flying MiG-23s and L-39s,

joined the Association officially as an honorary member during 1993. It has since disbanded, but its 'tiger' mantle has been taken up by 331.vrlt based at Prerov operating Mi-24 *Hind* attack helicopters, and the accession of the Czechs, Poles and Hungarians, along with the expansion of NATO's Partnership for Peace activities, is expected to bring further additions to the colourful Tiger community.

Above: The Portuguese Air Force has been represented in the Tiger Association by 301 Esquadra since 1978, a regular attendee at the Tiger Meets with specially painted aircraft – initially with this brilliantly painted Fiat G-91, but more recently with an Alpha Jet, currently on strength at Beja.

The Royal Navy provides the third of the UK's 'tiger' squadrons – 814 Naval Air Squadron, based at RNAS Culdrose. This Sea King HAS6 was suitably adorned for its attendance at the 1997 Tiger Meet.

Above: Cambrai based EC1/12 (now re-designated EC01.012) was one of the three original members of the Tiger Association and is today the only one of the three to be flying front line aircraft in Europe. This tiger-striped Mirage F1C has now been replaced by a Mirage 2000C, since the squadron re-equipped.

MEMBER SQUADRONS OF THE NATO TIGER ASSOCIATION IN 1999

Country	Air Arm	Unit	Equipment	Base	Date joined
Belgium	Force Aérienne Belge/ Belgische Luchtmacht	31 Smaldeel	F-16A/B	Kleine Brogel	1962
Czech Republic	Ceske Vojenske Letectvo	331.vrlt	Mi-24	Prerov	1997
France	Armée de l'Air	EC 01.012	Mirage 2000B/C	Cambrai	1961
		CEAM 05.330	Mirage 2000	Mont de Marsan	1990
	Aéronavale/Marine	11 Flotille	Super Etendard	Landivisiau	1979
Germany	Luftwaffe	1/JBG-32	Tornado ECR	Lechfeld	1996
		AKG-51	Tornado IDS	Schleswig-Jagel	1995
Italy	Aeronautica Militare Italiano	21° Gruppo	Tornado ADV	Cameri	1968
The Netherlands	Koninklijke Luchtmacht	313 Sqn	F-16A/B	Twenthe	1990
Norway	Kongelige Norske Luftvorsvaret	336 Skvadron	F-5A/B	Rygge	1977
Portugal	Força Aérea Portuguesa	301 Esquadra	Alpha Jet A	Beja	1978
Spain	Ejército del Aire	142 Escuadron	Mirage F1	Albacete	1986
Switzerland	Schweizer Luftwaffe	Flieger Staffel 11	F-5E	Dubendorf	1981
Turkey	Türk Hava Kuvvetleri	192 Filo	F-16C/D	Balikesir	1980
United Kingdom	Royal Air Force	74(R) Sqn	Hawk T1/T1A	RAF Valley	1961
		230 Sqn	Puma HC1	RAF Aldergrove	1977
	Royal Navy	814 NAS	Sea King HAS6	RNAS Culdrose	1979
United States	US Air Force	37th BS	B-1B	Ellsworth AFB	1997
		53rd FS*	F-15C/D	Spangdahlem AB	1962
		79th FS	F-16C/D	Shaw AFB	1961
		141st ARS	KC-135E	McGuire AFB	1991
		391st FS	F-15E	Mountain Home AFB	1962
		393rd BS	B-2A	Whiteman AFB	1978
		494th FS	F-15E	RAF Lakenheath	1997
	US Navy	VP-8	P-3C	NAS Brunswick	1979

* Unit disbanded in March 1999

Left: Tigers come in all shapes and sizes, and this close-up of the tail of a Dutch F-16A of 313 Squadron shows the care taken by the artist.

Below: This Royal Norwegian Air Force Northrop F-5A from 336 Squadron at Rygge was painted in tiger stripes right down to the wing-tip missiles and underwing drop-tanks when it attended the 1998 Tiger Meet at Cameri, Italy.

Right: While the UK has no Tornado 'tiger' squadrons, the Luftwaffe has two: 1/JBG-32 with Tornado ECRs at Lechfeld, and this colourful IDS from AKG-51 based at Schleswig-Jagel.

POSTSCRIPT

The Czech Republic, Hungary and Poland became the 17th, 18th and 19th member countries of NATO on 12 March 1999 when accession protocols were signed by the three foreign ministers in the Harry Truman Library at Independence, Missouri. Unfortunately, this significant development was immediately overshadowed by other events that took the Alliance into conflict as it approached its 50th anniversary.

Partial agreement on a political settlement for Kosovo, including deployment of a peacekeeping force, was reached on 23 February in talks at Rambouillet near Paris, and further negotiations were adjourned until 15 March. The British Prime Minister Tony Blair summed up the NATO view on 12 March: "Belgrade may choose to reject the agreement and/or launch a major offensive, leading to an overwhelming human catastrophe. NATO is prepared to take the necessary action to avert this. In this crucial period, President Milosevic and his commanders must understand that NATO will not stand by in the face of oppression and atrocities in Kosovo".

After four days of intensive negotiations following the resumption of talks on 15 March, the Kosovar Albanians accepted the accords, but the Serbs refused to sign. NATO's preparations for possible air strikes began in earnest, with numerous further aircraft deployments. As Serb forces carried out heavy attacks on ethnic Albanians in Kosovo, last-minute efforts by US negotiator Richard Holbrooke to avert military action failed, with Yugoslav President Milosevic opposing all demands for agreement. On 23 March, NATO Secretary General Javier Solana directed SACEUR, Gen. Wesley Clark, to begin operations against Yugoslavia. Under Operation *Allied Force*, NATO used its considerable air power to commence a bombardment of military targets in Serbia, Kosovo and Montenegro at 19.10 GMT on 24 March.

Having departed from RAF Fairford earlier that day, USAF B-52Hs from the 2nd Air Expeditionary Group participated in the initial wave of attacks with air-launched cruise missiles, backed up by Tomahawks fired from US Navy ships and the Royal Navy submarine HMS *Splendid* (the first time that Britain had launched cruise missiles in anger). The targets on the first night of *Allied Force* were mainly Yugoslav air defence installations, including airfields and radar sites, anti-aircraft artillery and SAM batteries. Also involved in the strikes on 24 March were Canadian Forces CF-188s, French Air Force Mirage 2000Ds, Spanish Air Force EF-18As, RAF Harrier GR7s, US Marine Corps F/A-18s, USAF A-10As, F-15Es, F-16Cs and F-117As and, for the first time, B-2s. All of the NATO aircraft involved in the first three nights' action returned safely to their bases in Italy, Britain and the USA.

Supporting NATO's strike force, F-16s from Belgium, Denmark, the Netherlands, Portugal and Turkey were among the aircraft providing air defence cover, while German Tornado ECRs and USMC EA-6Bs undertook SEAD and jamming duties amongst numerous combat support aircraft, that obviously included tankers. It is believed that 13 countries contributed to operations during the first three days of the *Allied Force* campaign.

US President Clinton confirmed on the second day that the bombing would continue until the Yugoslav leader was prepared to agree to a peaceful solution for Kosovo. Gen. Clark added that the bombardment would be 'severe, systematic and unrelenting'. These dramatic events were still continuing as the North Atlantic Treaty Organisation approached its 50th Anniversary.

PHOTO CREDITS

GLOSSARY

AAC	Army Air Corps
AAM	Air-to-Air Missile
AAR	Air-to-Air Refuelling
AAS	Aeromedical Airlift Squadron
AB	Air Base
AC	Army Co-operation
ACCS	Airborne Command and Control Squadron
ACDUCTRA	Active Duty Training
ACE	Allied Command Europe
ACF	Air Combat Fighter
AdlA	Armée de l'Air (French Air Force)
ADV	Air Defence Variant
Aeronautica Militare Italiana	Italian Air Force
Aéronavale	French Naval Aviation
AEW	Airborne Early Warning
AEW-SA	Air Expeditionary Wing Serbia
AF	Air Force
AFB	Air Force Base
AFCENT	Allied Forces Central Europe
AFRes	Air Force Reserve
AFSOUTH	Allied Forces Southern Europe
AJU	Ana Jet Us (Jet Air Base)
AKG	Aufklärungsgeschwader (Reconnaissance Wing)
Ala	Wing
AMF	Allied Command Europe Mobile Force
AMI	Aeronautica Militare Italiana (Italian Air Force)
AMRAAM	Advanced Medium-Range Air-to-Air Missile
Ana Jet Us	Jet Air Base
ANG	Air National Guard
APU	Auxiliary Power Unit
ARGE	Arbeitsgemeinschaft (Working Group)
Armée de l'Air	French Air Force
ARW	Air Refueling Wing
AS	Airlift Squadron
ASA	Aggiornamento Sistema d'Arma (Weapons Systems Upgrade)
ASTOR	Advanced Stand-off Radar
ASTOVL	Advanced Short Take-off and Vertical Landing
ASW	Anti-Submarine Warfare
ATAF	Allied Tactical Air Force
Aufklärungsgeschwader	Reconnaissance Wing
AW&CS	Airborne Warning and Control Squadron
AWACS	Airborne Warning and Control System
BA	Brigata Aerea (Air Brigade)
BAC	British Aircraft Corporation
BAe	British Aerospace
BMW	Bayerische Motorenwerke
Brigada	Brigade
Bundesmarine	Federal German Navy
Bundeswehr	German Armed Forces
BW	Bombardment Wing
C-in-C	Commander-in-Chief
CAD	Canadian Air Division
CAF	Canadian Armed Forces
CAP	Combat Air Patrol
CASA	Construcciones Aeronautics SA
CEAM	Centre d'Expérimentation Aériennes Militaires (Military Air Experimental Centre)
CFB	Canadian Forces Base
CFE	Conventional Forces in Europe
CIA	Central Intelligence Agency
CIMIC	Civil-Military Co-operation
CIS	Commonwealth of Independent States
Commandement Aérien Tactique	Tactical Air Command
CTOL	Conventional Take-off and Landing
CzAF	Czech Air Force
DDR	Deutsche Demokratische Republic (German Democratic Republic)
DH	de Havilland
EB	Escadron de Bombardement (Bombardment Wing)
EC	Escadron de Chasse (Fighter Wing)
ECR	Electronic Combat Reconnaissance
ECS	Electronic Combat Squadron
ECTT	Escadre de Chasse Tous-Temps (All-Weather Fighter Wing)
EdA	Ejercito del Aire (Spanish Air Force)
EdCA	Escadron de Détection et de Control Aéroportée (Airborne Detection and Control Squadron)
EE	Escadron Electronique (Electronic Warfare Squadron)
EH	Escadron d'Helicoptères (Helicopter Squadron)
ELINT	Electronic Intelligence
ER	Escadron de Reconnaissance (Reconnaissance Squadron)
ERS	Escadre de Reconnaissance Stratégique (Strategic Reconnaissance Wing/Expeditionary Reconnaissance Squadron)
ERV	Escadron de Ravitaillement en Vol (In-Flight Refuelling Squadron)
Esc	Escadron (Squadron)
Escadron de Chasse	Fighter Wing
Esk	Eskadrille (Squadron)
Eskadrille	Squadron
Esq	Esquadra (Squadron)
Esquadra	Squadron
EWR	Entwicklungsring
FIAR	Fabbrica Italiana Apparecchiatture Radioelettriche
Filo	Squadron
FIS	Fighter Interceptor Squadron
FLA	Future Large Aircraft/Airbus A400M
Flieger Staffel	Squadron
Flotille	Naval Air Wing
FOL	Forward Operating Location
FRG	Federal Republic of Germany
FS	Fighter Squadron
FSD	Full-Scale Development
FW	Fighter Wing
GC	Groupe de Chasse (Fighter Group)
GE	Groupement Ecole (Flying Training School)
Geschwader	Wing
Gruppo	Squadron
HARM	High-speed Anti-Radiation Missile
HC	Helicopter Combat Support Squadron
HFS	Heeresfliegerstaffel (Helicopter Squadron)
HMS	Her Majesty's Ship
HQ	Headquarters
HS	Hawker Siddeley/Helicopter Squadron
ICBM	Intercontinental Ballistic Missile
ICE	Improved Combat Efficiency
ICTY	International Criminal Tribunal for the Former Yugoslavia
IDS	Interdictor Strike
IFOR	Implementation Force
INF	Intermediate Nuclear Force
J-STARS	Joint Surveillance Target Attack Radar System
Jagdbombergeschwader	Fighter-Bomber Wing
Jagdgeschwader	Fighter Wing
JBG	Jagdbombergeschwader (Fighter-Bomber Wing)
JG	Jagdgeschwader (Fighter Wing)
JSF	Joint Strike Fighter
KLA	Kosovo Liberation Army
KLu	Koninklijke Luchtmacht (Royal Netherlands Air Force)
km	Kilometres
KNL	Kongelige Norske Luftforsvaret (Royal Norwegian Air Force)
LANTIRN	Low-Altitude Navigation and Targeting Infra-Red for Night
LeKG	Leicht Kampfgeschwader (Light Attack Squadron)
Letka	Squadron
LGB	Laser-Guided Bomb
LSK/LV	Luftstreitkräfte und Luftverteidigung (East German Air Forces and Air Defence)
LTDP	Long-Term Defence Plan
LTG	Lufttransportgeschwader (Air Transport Wing)
LTS	Lufttransportstaffel (Air Transport Squadron)
Luftwaffe	German Air Force

LWF	Lightweight Fighter		SFOR	Stabilisation Force
MAC	Military Airlift Command		SHAPE	Supreme Headquarters Allied Powers Europe
Marinefliegergeschwader	Naval Air Wing		Skv	Skvadron (Squadron)
MATS	Military Air Transport Service		Skvadron	Squadron
MBB	Messerschmitt Bolkow-Blohm		SLP	Stíhací Letecké Pluk (Fighter Wing)
MBFR	Mutual Balanced Force Reductions		slt	stíhací letka (Fighter Squadron)
MC	Military Concept		Smaldeel	Squadron
MD	Marcel Dassault		Sml	Smaldeel (Squadron)
MDAP	Mutual Defense Assistance Program		SNCASE	Société Nationale de Constructions Aéronautiques
MFG	Marinefliegergeschwader (Naval Air Wing)			du Sud-Ouest
MiG	Mikoyan-Gurevich		SOS	Special Operations Squadron
Mira	Squadron		Sqn	Squadron
MIRSIP	Mirage Systems Improvement Programme		SRW	Strategic Reconnaissance Wing
MLU	Mid-Life Update		Staffel	Squadron
MNCAOC	Multinational Combined Air Operations Center		STANAVFORLANT	Standing Naval Force Atlantic
MND/N	Multinational Division North		STANAVFORMED	Standing Naval Force Mediterranean
MND/SE	Multinational Division South-East		START	Strategic Arms Reduction Treaty
MND/SW	Multinational Division South-West		Stormo	Wing
MR	Maritime Reconnaissance		TAC	Tactical Air Command
MRCA	Multi-Role Combat Aircraft		TACEVAL	Tactical Evaluation
MTU	Motor Turbo Union		TAM	Tactical Air Meet
NACC	North Atlantic Co-operation Council		TARPS	Tactical Air Reconnaissance Pod System
NAEWF	NATO Airborne Early Warning Force		TDY	Temporary Duty
NAF	Naval Air Facility		TFS	Tactical Fighter Squadron
NAS	Naval Air Station/Naval Air Squadron		TFW	Tactical Fighter Wing
NATO	North Atlantic Treaty Organisation		TFX	Tactical Fighter Experimental
NBMR	NATO Basic Military Requirement		TIALD	Thermal Imaging and Laser Designation
NFTC	NATO Flying Training in Canada		TLP	Tactical Leadership Programme
NFZ	No-Fly Zone		TOW	Tactical Optical Warfare
NORAD	North American Air Defence		TRW	Tactical Reconnaissance Wing
OCU	Operational Conversion Unit		TTTE	Tri-National Tornado Training Establishment
OSCE	Organisation for Security and Co-operation in Europe		TWCU	Tornado Weapons Conversion Unit
PfP	Partnership for Peace		UAV	Unmanned Aerial Vehicle
PLM	Pulk Lotnictwa Mysliwskego (Air Fighter Regiment)		UKADR	United Kingdom Air Defence Region
PRU	Photographic Reconnaissance Unit		UN	United Nations
PVO	Protivovozdushnoy Oborony (Troops of Air Defence)		UNHCR	United Nations High Commissioner for Refugees
PZL	Panstwowe Zaklady Lotnicze		UNPROFOR	United Nations Protection Force
QRA	Quick Reaction Alert		USAF	United States Air Force
R-R	Rolls-Royce		USAFE	United States Air Forces Europe
RAF	Royal Air Force		USEUCOM	United States European Command
RCAF	Royal Canadian Air Force		USMC	United States Marine Corps
Reparto Sperimentale Volo	Experimental Flight Centre		USN	United States Navy
RHC	Régiment d'Helicoptères de Combat		USS	United States Ship
	(Combat Helicopter Regiment)		USSR	Union of Soviet Socialist Republics
RHCM	Régiment d'Helicoptères de Commandement		VA	Virginia or Attack Squadron
	et de Manoeuvre		VAK	Vertikalstartendes Aufklärungs-und Kampfflugzeug
	(Command & Transport Helicopter Regiment)			(Vertical Take-off Reconnaissance and Attack Aircraft)
RN	Royal Navy		VAQ	Tactical Electronic Warfare Squadron
RRF	Rapid Reaction Force		VAW	Carrier Airborne Early Warning Squadron
RS	Reconnaissance Squadron		VF	Fighter Squadron
RW	Reconnaissance Wing		VFA	Strike Fighter Squadron
Saab	Svenska Aeroplan Aktieboleg		VFW	Vereinigte Flugtechnische Werke
SABCA	Société Anonyme Belge de Constructions		VMAQ	Marine Tactical Electronic Warfare Squadron
	Aeronautiques		VMFA	Marine Fighter Attack Squadron
SAC	Strategic Air Command		VMFA(AW)	Marine All-weather Fighter Attack Squadron
SACEUR	Supreme Allied Commander Europe		VP	Patrol Squadron
SALT	Strategic Arms Limitation Treaty		VQ	Fleet Air Reconnaissance Squadron
SAM	Surface-to-Air Missile		vrlt	vrtulníkového letka (Helicopter Squadron)
SAR	Search and Rescue		VS	Air Anti-submarine Squadron
SAS	Special Air Service		V/STOL	Vertical/short take-off and landing
Schiessplatzstaffel	Target-Towing Squadron		VTOL	Vertical take-off and landing
SDI	Strategic Defense Initiative		Waffenausbildungs-komponente	Weapons Training Component
SDR	Strategic Defence Review		Wg	Wing
SEAD	Suppression of Enemy Air Defences		WS	Waffenschule (Weapons School)
SED	Sozialistische Einheitspartei Deutschlands		WTD	Wehrtechnische Dienstelle (Technical Support Unit)
	(East German Communist Party)		WU	Western Union
SEPECAT	Société Européenne de Production de l'Avion Ecole		WW2	World War Two
	de Combat et d'Appui Tactique		ZELL	Zero-Length Launch